What people are saying about

The Beginner's Guide to Managing

Mikil has done a remarkable job of creating a simple and actionable blueprint to guide new managers. It is very well written with easily relatable examples and common sense advice. I would recommend *The Beginner'* _____ *Managing* to everyone moving into their first mar_____
Brian Moyer, President & CEO _____ _____ _____ 'nology Council

Nothing replaces experien_____ _____ . Mikil Taylor's new book comes very close. In _____ you'll find the answers derived from his own person_____ _____perience as a new manager as he learned from others and from his own mistakes along the way. Leading others is a challenging and even scary undertaking but with Mikil's wisdom from these pages you can shortcut your own path and save yourself plenty of struggle along the way. Dive in and get better faster!
Andy Bailey, Founder, Petra Coach, and Author of *No Try Only Do*

The Beginner's Guide to Managing is a thoughtful analysis for first-time managers. My first time managing a technical group in healthcare was at a Fortune 50 corporation. People often referred to the «Peter Principle» in our company. I was bound and determined not to show my incompetence. Fortunately for me, I had an excellent mentor who guided my path through a structured process while I learned on the job. *The Beginner's Guide to Managing* will help new managers avoid many pitfalls new managers experience.
J. Tod Fetherling, Author and Speaker, CEO, Perception Health

Mikil's innate generosity shines through in this guide for managers. He begins with the need to treat your team with love and that foundation continues throughout each chapter. Even if you've been a manager for many years, this book will raise your game.

Jeffrey Rice, MD, JD, Founder and Executive Chairman, Healthcare Bluebook

Novice technical managers should definitely read this!

Fred Trotter, CTO, CareSet Labs

The Beginner's Guide to Managing is a must read for anyone looking for a refreshing, simple, and actionable guide to the fundamentals of leadership. Mikil is a unique new voice in the world of Business Management theory; a voice that will benefit those new to leadership grappling with their role, or those with years of experience looking to refresh their approach.

John M. Anderson, Partner, Resource Communications Group, and Co-creator of the Nashville Technology Council - Emerging Leader in Technology and Engineering (ELITE) Program

Every good book needs to be impactful. Mikil's book brings managing people into focus by allowing new managers to use his experience and insight to learn fewer lessons the hard way. It also allows them to focus on some of the big questions every manager has to decide about their management style. This book is required reading for all new managers in my company.

Charlie Yielding, CEO, G Squared Wireless

The Beginner's Guide to Managing provides an in depth guide to get new team leaders up to speed in all aspects of their new role. This handy primer will save years of pain and suffering of learning how to manage a team via trial and error. This indispensable book covers the gamut of leadership topics; managing your team, managing your bosses, and managing yourself. While most leadership books focus myopically on managing your team, Mikil touches all bases of a leader's job, including figuring out what work should be prioritized to begin with.

Brian Johnson, Co-Founder, DonorBureau, LLC

Honest, vulnerable, direct and hugely valuable – all describe the author, as well as his latest gift for first-time managers. If you find yourself dropped on the Island of New Managers, this is your survival kit – portable, water-proof, capable of starting a fire and securing food for you and your team. In short, everything you need (and nothing you don't) to survive your first 90 days on The Island of New Managers – and ultimately, thrive.

Michael O'Neil, Sheepdog, Healthcare Bluebook

Mikil's book is impressive and refreshing, packing a lot of timely information into a succinct and quick read. While the title accurately suggests this is a book for beginning managers, it also has key principles that are relevant at any stage. While it targets the manager, this book has timeless lessons for aspirational and seasoned leaders. As I near four decades of my professional journey, I found key words of wisdom that help me continue to grow in my leadership journey.

Andy Flatt, SVP/CIO, National Healthcare Corp, 36 Year Healthcare and Technology Executive

The Beginner's Guide to Managing

A Guide to the Toughest Journey
You'll Ever Take

The Beginner's Guide to Managing

A Guide to the Toughest Journey You'll Ever Take

Mikil Taylor

BUSINESS
BOOKS

Winchester, UK
Washington, USA

JOHN HUNT PUBLISHING

First published by Business Books, 2021
Business Books is an imprint of John Hunt Publishing Ltd., No. 3 East St., Alresford,
Hampshire SO24 9EE, UK
office@jhpbooks.com
www.johnhuntpublishing.com
www.johnhuntpublishing.com/business-books

For distributor details and how to order please visit the 'Ordering' section on our website.

Text copyright: Mikil Taylor 2020

ISBN: 978 1 78904 583 3
978 1 78904 584 0 (ebook)
Library of Congress Control Number: 2020930845

All rights reserved. Except for brief quotations in critical articles or reviews, no part of this
book may be reproduced in any manner without prior written permission from the publishers.

The rights of Mikil Taylor as author have been asserted in accordance with the Copyright,
Designs and Patents Act 1988.

A CIP catalogue record for this book is available from the British Library.

Design: Stuart Davies

Printed and bound by CPI Group (UK) Ltd, Croydon, CR0 4YY

We operate a distinctive and ethical publishing philosophy in
all areas of our business, from our global network of authors to
production and worldwide distribution.

Contents

Acknowledgements

I first need to thank those who helped me with the writing process itself. Writing *The Beginner's Guide to Managing* took dedication and perseverance, and many times my writing was less clear than I intended. Charlie Yielding really helped me to make sure my intended meaning translated by letting me see the book through someone else's eyes. Katie Burdette helped to run through a round of copyediting to catch all the words I missed when my brain was working faster than my word processor. Heather Botting was an incredible asset as an editor, and the book is dramatically more readable and clear as a direct result of her work.

WRVU Radio at Vanderbilt University was my first real experience as a manager, and clearly illustrated my shortcomings, many of which I would struggle with in my professional career. It was a wonderful learning experience, and everyone there helped my growth in ways large and small.

I want to thank everyone involved with the NTC ELITE Program, but especially John Anderson, Meg Chamblee, Suzi Earhart, Joanne Eckton, Andy Flatt, and Jacqui Logan.

I also want to thank former managers at previous jobs: Nancy Dion, Jim Hayes, Serim Huh, Jacob Larvie, and Ruth Mothorpe.

Doug Traxler has been a wonderful friend and resource, and has helped me to clarify my thinking on a number of topics related to management.

Andy Bailey at Petra Coach has shaped a lot of my thinking on how to effectively get things done, and his influence is felt throughout the book.

The leadership team at Healthcare Bluebook, especially Jeff Rice, Bill Kampine, and Erik Nicholson who took a shot on a reformed actuary to help grow their startup, and Mike O'Neil, Rick Leach, Amy Moore, and Will Brockman have all been invaluable advisers and resources over the years.

I also want to thank everyone I've had the opportunity to directly manage. Some of these lessons were only learned through trial and error, and I appreciate your patience with me as I learned how to be a good manager. Hopefully this book will help guide you as well.

Jason Turan has been an incredibly helpful influence on me as a manager, and it's fair to say that this book would not exist without his guidance and influence. He has consistently been there to help me put theory into practice, and to tackle tough problems. Zack Samples has also had a similar influence on me, and I will always be indebted to him for his training, support, and guidance.

My father in law Donnie Drayton has been a valuable voice as I have entered my career, and is consistently helpful and there when needed.

My mom has shaped the person I am today, and she along with my brother and sisters keeps me tied to who I am and where I came from.

My dad passed away in 2017 after a long battle with cancer, but there is nobody I try harder to emulate. I wish he could read this.

Lastly and most importantly is my wife Sarah. I could write another book expressing how much she means to me. She inspires me to be a better person. This book wouldn't exist without her, because I wouldn't be worthy of writing it. She has given direction and purpose to my life, and there is nobody whose opinion I trust more. She is the rock of my life, and the one I do everything for.

Introduction

Like many first-time managers, my introduction to my role was a disaster.

The decision to promote me to a manager was logical, well-considered, and maybe even overdue. I had been at my company for over four years, working my way up from a junior analyst to become a critical linchpin of not only the team, but to hear my boss describe it, the entire company. I had trained most of the team members, and already functioned as an effective team lead. I was ready to go.

Within three months, half my team had left and I was scrambling for answers.

Many missteps later, I became an effective manager of an award-winning team. Am I perfect, or do I make the right decisions all the time? Absolutely not! A fantastic week still contains multiple mistakes and decisions I'd make differently in hindsight. But I believe that I can help you avoid some of the mistakes I made during my early time as a manager.

According to Harvard Business Review, 85% of first-time managers believe they were not given the support and training they needed as a first-time manager. This book is aimed squarely at those ambitious men and women who want to take the solution into their own hands, but don't know the right tools to use.

I prefer short, direct, practical guides instead of windy articles filled with theory about how "the world of work is changing." The best way to become a good manager is to try to be a good manager, so this book will point you in the right direction and leave it to you to actually go and implement the suggestions and strategies. Reading this book and not taking action is just a waste of everyone's time, so unless you're committed to taking action, please put the book down and go do something more productive.

I'll bet you've had a terrible boss in the past. Think about how they made you feel, and how coming into work day after day was close to self-inflicted torture. Those people were once first-time managers too. The only difference between them and you is that you recognize that you might be a terrible manager, and want to change.

Let's dive in.

Chapter 1

Managing With Love

I've lost half of you already. You're probably flipping to the back cover of the book to double-check the synopsis. Seeing who the publisher is to see if it's one of those "Christian" self-help books. Or maybe this is some kind of hippie thing?

Unfortunately, you're stuck. You have the book already, either because you chose to buy it or because your boss told you to check it out. While you're here, come along with me.

Why would I lead off a book with a piece about love, and what on earth does it have to do with managing people?

It's because you've been tricked. You've probably started reading this book hoping for some strategies for how to successfully tell others what to do. This book isn't about three easy steps to take your new team from dysfunctional to spectacular. It can't teach you the magic words to make that one emotional person stop crying all the time or for that salesman to stop being a jerk to everyone. You won't be able to cajole and threaten your team to behave, because this book is about you and your attitude. Instead of trying to change others, the point is to understand yourself.

In fact, I guarantee that you won't learn anything from this book unless you internalize and truly believe this one sentence. Treat everyone with love.

Yes, I heard the record scratch in your head. To clarify, I am not talking about romancing all of your employees. Please, please, please don't do that.

What I mean when I say love can also be referred to as brotherly love, empathy, kindness, caring, and a million other words.

When you ask someone a question, you're concentrating on

their answer, not your response.

When training someone, you're concentrating on their growth and learning, not your lack of time.

When correcting behavior, you're concentrating on their mindset, not your annoyance.

When celebrating an accomplishment, you're concentrating on the growth they've shown, not how this will reflect on you.

When hiring or firing someone, you're concentrating on their life goals and fit, not how this affects your job.

This is the mindset of successful leaders. If you want someone to follow you, you must first follow them.

Of course, just because this is an ideal mindset doesn't mean it's the only mindset. In fact, you can be successful without "managing with love," and you probably already have some people in mind who were able to do this.

Don't base your management style on their example. They took the easy way, and managed to succeed. What you don't see are the hundreds of people who tried to manage the same way, but have failed and continue to fail.

This happens in life all the time. Some people manage to succeed without doing things ""the right way." Some basketball players get to the NBA without passing to their teammates. Some investors make millions without properly accounting for risk. Some high school students get into Ivy League schools without working hard. Their success should not be taken as a lesson, because you don't see the countless failures who took the same approach.

Remember too that you're not just trying to reach this position. You're trying to do well when you get there. Habits that you establish now will hang around and become part of your management style, so it's worth the effort to make sure those habits are positive and not negative.

If you truly care about doing your job well, you want to know that your efforts have a good chance of success. You don't coast along with "good enough." When you take on a project, you take its success as a personal mission and its failure just as personally. You get things done, which is why you got promoted in the first place.

Becoming a manager for the first time is one of the most difficult transitions you'll make in your career. Most of the skills and habits that made you qualified for the promotion are now irrelevant, and doubling down on them is counterproductive. If you are fantastic at finding bugs in code, you may be able to teach someone else how to do that, but you won't automatically have the skills to manage that person. You need to learn new skills and habits, and successful implementation of those habits requires a team that has your back. If you want that, you have to first demonstrate that you have their backs, and that you care about them as people.

If you continually approach discussions with your team in a "me-focused" mindset, it will not be a secret. Even if the team can't articulate it, they will understand how they feel about it. And if they know you're only concerned with yourself, it's really easy for them to disregard coaching, correction, and guidance, because if you don't understand and love them, you can't communicate effectively with them. If they disregard the most important things you tell them (and your coaching, correction, and guidance are thousands of times more important for an employee than task assignment), then you can't expect a high-performing team. They must trust you.

As a manager, you are your team. If your team is successful, you will be successful. If they fail, you will fail, too. And no matter how hard you try, you cannot force a team to work better. Perversely, trying harder usually produces the opposite effect. You have to win your team to your vision and your priorities. If you can do that, then they will work for you, rather than against you.

And to do that, you have to treat everyone with love.

Now that you've read the first chapter, you're released. You can stop, tell your coworkers that this book is a bunch of hokey nonsense, and feel good in your decision.

Oh, and one more thing.

Try one exercise over the next few days. Chat with a coworker you don't normally interact with, and ask them about hobbies they've been pursuing lately. As they start to explain sewing or biking or chicken-raising, listen deeply. Don't think about your hobbies or how that reminds you of a funny story that you're just dying to tell. Stay focused on them. Ask them questions. If they talk about their new guitar, ask them how they decided to pick that particular model. If they just got back from Disney World, ask about their favorite parts of the park. The key is to focus on them and express deep interest.

Later, think back on that conversation. How many of the following apply to you? 1) You know that person better, 2) You feel great, 3) You've got more energy, and 4) Your brain is working overtime.

If you're anything like most people, it's all four. That's the feeling that managing with love will give you and your team.

Chapter 2

Making Your Team Look Good

Most first-time managers are promoted to management because of the outstanding quality of their work. They've become the go-to resource for multiple people in the organization because nobody has to question their output, knowledge, or advice. When there is a question, it's answered promptly and thoroughly. The soon-to-be manager rightfully takes pride in the high quality and consistency of their work.

Once promoted, the new manager owns a team's worth of work. Some of it is routine, some of it is unimportant noise, and some of it is critical and urgent. No matter how divided, there is more work than one person can do. Now they are expected to juggle all of these tasks and ensure that everything is done to a high standard. With little training in how to do this for a team's worth of work, new managers often swerve wildly between two ways of managing important work: micromanaging and over-delegating.

1. Micromanaging. They try to do everything important themselves, or at least undertake a lengthy auditing process before proclaiming someone else's work "done." Since the team's work reflects on the leader, the most important thing is making sure it's held to high standards.
2. Over-delegating. They try to remove themselves entirely from the work product. Requests come in the door, are immediately assigned to a subordinate, and eventually get finished. This is, after all, what delegating is.

Both strategies are valid ways of organizing specific projects, and you will have to understand when and how to use each one. Deciding which one to use is often a complex recipe that incorporates employee competence, task difficulty, task importance, task visibility, and a million other considerations. You will end up making the wrong choice sometimes. Even very experienced managers can misjudge whether they should dive into the details or leave them to their team.

There is a helpful framework you can use when you're confronted by this choice of whether to handle a task yourself or give it to someone else. The key is to realize that your role as a manager is to make the name of each member of your team synonymous with high-quality work, just like your name was and is.

Ask yourself, "What can I do to make this person look good?" You want to put them in a position where they can do their best work and receive the credit for doing it. Some employees may only be able to do small tasks well, while others may be even more capable than you are. You should work to know your team well enough to assign them work that they are capable of doing, and that will help them grow. To do this, you will need to understand what each person on your team does well and where they are likely to have trouble.

Consider the following scenario:

You are the IT manager for a small retail company, and part of your team's responsibility is to run the store website. Your boss wants to know why the website was slow over the weekend. As soon as the question is asked, you know that John, one of your team members, is who you want to look into it.

John has an intuitive feel for how the site works and you know that he can uncover the problem. Unfortunately, he has difficulty taking a complex technical problem and explaining it to a non-technical person. He has a tendency to focus on arcane details, and you know that he would mostly just confuse your boss. Normally, you would have him research the problem, explain the answer to you, and you translate before sending it along to your boss.

But what if you think about it in terms of "What will make John look good?" He's already fully capable of diagnosing and understanding the problem, so you probably can't be any additional help there. But he needs substantial help in putting it into words that your boss can understand. This is where you can help him grow, since clear communication is always helpful if you want to advance in an organization.

If you take time to work on John's explanation with him, you have an opportunity to highlight his problem-solving skills in front of your boss. While John is explaining the solution to you, ask him to help you translate it into a three-sentence "boss-friendly" explanation. The two of you work together to land on the best wording. You may feel like you're contributing a lot of the explanation, and that's okay at first. You're demonstrating how you think through the issue of translation from tech-speak into boss-speak.

Once the two of you have a good plan, leave him alone to make a draft and send it to you. This is a good chance for him to think privately about how to answer it, which some employees will find easier since there's less pressure. Once he sends the draft, review it. If you find it needs substantial revision, don't make the changes yourself. Go back and consult with him on how to fix those pieces, and have him send you an update. Once you've got a good draft, make any final polishes you need and send it along to your boss, with a short additional note praising John by name for figuring out the issue and writing the explanation. Make sure you copy John in on the email as well.

If you do this, you have accomplished multiple things. You have trained your employee on a skill he needs but doesn't have, you have publicly praised him for the great skills he already possesses, and you've done it all in the context of normal day-to-day business rather than an artificial training course. Everyone appreciates having their good work recognized, and it's more meaningful to praise good performance when it happens in the course of their job rather than after completing an online assessment.

The more you help your team, the more independent they will become. At some point, you'll ask them to explain a problem to you or draft an email to send along, and they'll respond with something better than you could have done yourself. This is a really exciting time, and you should share that excitement with them. Be generous with your praise.

This is just one example of how to help make a member of your team look good, but the principle holds no matter their strengths or weaknesses. Consider a rookie employee, Jean, who is pretty good at communicating but not strong on the technical side yet. You trust Jean to articulate her findings clearly, but she doesn't understand the systems well enough to diagnose the problem accurately. Just like with the email draft, you have to help guide her through the skills she needs to improve. Show her how you think through the problem, but let her do the actual work. Once the issue has been resolved, you may have contributed a significant portion of the answer. Again, that's okay at first. You're not here to take credit, you're here to show her how to excel in her job.

Objections

I imagine you have a lot of questions, and I've tried to anticipate some of them below.

This Takes Too Much Time

Unfortunately, there is no magic formula for spending one-on-one time with your employees on a time budget. Training people well takes time and it takes effort. The investment that you make today will pay off tremendously over time as your employees are able to own tasks that previously were only doable by you. If you don't make the investment today, your team will not grow, your workload will not decrease, and your time problem will only get worse. Time you invest in your team today will provide everyone with significant benefits in the future.

Won't Their Gain Hurt Me?

I see this line of thinking occasionally from junior employees, and some senior ones. The idea is that everyone is competing for a few promotions or raises, so the most logical course of action is to try to stand out as the best. If this is your goal, then helping to push others to the forefront doesn't make any sense.

There is a kernel of truth to this line of thinking. A team cannot consist exclusively of managers, and money is a finite resource within any company. However, this obscures the real practical truth of the matter. If you consistently produce a high-achieving team, it will be clear to all involved that you are a primary reason for the success. If you consistently produce a team of individuals who can't produce independently, it will also be clear to all involved that you are a primary cause. If you want to be a good manager, you have to let your team excel.

Isn't It My Accomplishment Too?

Your accomplishment is the competent management of your team. No manager can be good unless their team is well managed, even if individual tasks are done well. You don't need to fish for praise for tasks, because tasks are a secondary part of your job.

This Isn't Worth Praising, Because It's So Easy

Easy to you is not the same as easy to them. You also had to learn these skills, and probably had trouble with a number of them. You are not a snooty film critic trying to be the final arbiter of quality. You are training an employee, and it's good to recognize their growth, even if other people are currently better than them.

Wouldn't a "Sink or Swim" Approach Be Better?

Many people have learned by "Sink or Swim" and have stories of being thrown into a difficult job with no guidance or help. Despite the fact that you've overcome the challenge, it's not actually a good way to train someone.

Consider whether your goal is to make a point, or to make the team better. Because "Sink or Swim" is only best for making a point. Throwing someone into a task with no guidance or training and assuming they will eventually figure it out is a slower, riskier, and less effective way to train your team. Even if they do succeed, they will only have their own perspective to judge their success or failure, and most people are blind to their weaknesses. Your team will need to work independently, but you do not have to let them work without a guide.

Final Thoughts

As a manager, the most fundamental thing for you to understand is that your team's success is your success. Your job is to facilitate their victories. You put them in a position to succeed and grow, and you applaud wildly when they do. If your team is making great strides and growing, then you will be seen as the person facilitating that process. If your team is stagnating and consistently making the same mistakes, then you will also be seen as the person responsible. Having a team that is continually improving is the ultimate achievement.

Remember, this will fail horribly unless you approach your team with a spirit of love and goodwill. If you genuinely want them to succeed and grow, then you will be rewarded with a team of individuals who are excited about taking on new challenges and growing by leaps and bounds. If you approach this in a transactional way, it will be obvious to your people that you are not personally invested in them. If you coach with a spirit of defensiveness or impatience, it will not be effective. If you are frustrated that your employees don't know everything already, they will be less receptive to your ideas. Don't forget that you also had to learn these skills, and you may have had the advantage of a great manager or very clear insight into your own weaknesses. Be forgiving and gracious, and this spirit will help move your team forward.

Chapter 3

Setting An Example

You were probably promoted to a management position because you're really good at getting things done. You demonstrate creativity and tenacity in solving problems, so your track record is impressive. It was a no-brainer to have you lead a team that does similar work.

But now you're being measured by your teams' track record rather than just your own. Unfortunately, they may not always be up to your standard, particularly when you are just starting out. This can be an especially frustrating time for a lot of new managers because their top-notch individual work product isn't automatically translating into top-notch work from the team. You need to train your team to look at problems in the same way you do and to meet your standard.

Parenting

Managing is a lot like parenting. When you're doing it for the first time, suddenly your world changes from you-focused to others-focused. With parenting, there's no shortage of advice from parents, friends, neighbors, and even strangers, plus you have examples from books, movies, TV, and the Internet to use as a guide for what you should be doing (or not doing). If you aren't sure how to handle a situation, someone you know has dealt with it before and will gladly give you advice.

Of course, parenting and managing differ dramatically in the scale of responsibility, but their similarities can still be useful to consider. Let's walk through some examples, keeping in mind that you don't actually have to send your employees to college or pack their lunches.

Shaping behavior is a part of every manager's job, and one of the most difficult things for new managers to wrap their heads around. If a child is breaking things or being mean to friends, a good parent will notice and correct the behavior, explain why it is a problem, and make sure it doesn't happen again. If your team member is treating coworkers poorly or missing important deadlines, then as a good manager this is bad behavior you must correct. You have to let them know that their behavior is unacceptable and make a plan for fixing it.

Noticing and correcting this bad behavior comes naturally to a lot of parents, but new managers can sometimes be nervous about correcting someone's work. It can be really easy to notice someone else's errors and have a desire to hold their feet to the fire, but actually confronting another adult doesn't always come naturally. This is why your attitude toward your team is critical. Like a parent, your main motivation should be for the wellbeing of your employees. Approaching this confrontation as someone who is genuinely trying to help doesn't guarantee it will always go smoothly, but it does make it a lot more likely.

It takes practice to do this kindly and compassionately. People naturally get defensive when shown their errors, which makes it harder to have a simple and honest conversation. Deliver the feedback privately rather than in a group setting. Public criticism is especially embarrassing for most people and will cause the recipient to resent you. If your goal is to improve their behavior, you need the criticism to be taken to heart. This is difficult to do if they resent you for embarrassing them.

Get their side of the story first. Ask them to start by explaining the situation to you, and hold your comments until they're finished explaining. To make sure your message lands, you have to give them a chance to be heard. In doing so, you will often hear them point out their own errors before you even start speaking.

Regardless, hold a compassionate but firm line on what is and isn't acceptable. When a parent misses an opportunity to shape behavior, they prolong the existence of that behavior. Same thing for managers. Address issues quickly and consistently to hold your team to an acceptable standard of behavior.

Other responsibilities are a little more complex and nuanced. For example, you need to set clear expectations before those problems arise. Some expectations are globally recognized, such as treating others kindly, but others are more specific to the individual, family, or team.

For example, some families make it a point to eat meals together with no distractions, while others couldn't care less about family dinner time. Some teams place heavy emphasis on the quality of their work, while others make a bigger deal about completing tasks on time. Regardless of what specific expectations you have, they need to be well-known, explicit, and consistently enforced. Otherwise, you are asking your team to try to hit a target that they cannot see or that keeps moving.

But how can you possibly expect to have all of these expectations written down? It's impossible to create a comprehensive legal framework to govern the behavior of your team or family. Even if you could, you probably shouldn't. Just because rules are written in a document somewhere does not mean that people will remember their details or that they exist. Being technically correct when pointing out someone's error doesn't win you any points if your team doesn't remember the written rules. You need to find a way to make sure your team clearly understands what is okay and what is not.

A very effective way to do this is to set out clear principles that explain the most important guidelines. These guidelines play an important role in setting boundaries for you to shape behavior. Keep the list of guidelines short, otherwise no one will remember it.

Ultimately, what makes the parenting analogy for managers work or fail is your attitude toward your team. You can think about your team as replaceable employees who don't exist outside of work hours, or you can think about them as a group placed under your responsibility and care, with the expectation that you will nurture them to grow into something spectacular. I recognize that some companies refuse to take this responsibility and discourage their managers from getting too attached to their team, but they are wrong. You have been given a role that will allow you to help others, so take advantage of it, and be the best leader you can be.

Explicit Work Standards

Teams have many different examples of how to describe their culture, and most don't write it down, preferring to let it live in the mind of the leader and be absorbed by the rest of the team. This is the easiest path to take, but it's a lot more likely to stick with your team and actually guide their work if it's written down and given to them.

Below are a few examples of standards different teams use. Decide which ones you're already trying to get the team to adhere to. Would it be helpful to make the expectation explicit?

Either
- Our work reflects on us and needs to be clean and free of errors, even if it takes twice as long.

Or
- Finished is better than perfect.

Either
- We are scaling as fast as we can, so we will not do work that doesn't scale.

Or
- Our existing customers are where our revenue comes from, so we need to concentrate on their needs to make sure we don't lose them.

Either
- Always be closing.

Or

- Building a relationship with the customer is more important than today's sale.

There are many more examples of the behavior that different teams find important to emphasize, but hopefully these examples give you some insight into your own thinking and behavior, making clear what you expect from your team.

Demonstrating Behavior

Now for the most difficult responsibility: You have to demonstrate the desired behavior yourself. You're probably thinking that you do this already, since you're the one setting the standards. That is probably true most of the time. These are things important to you, so you're going to hold yourself to them. But think harder. Are you truly as good as you think you are about being kind to your team? About meeting deadlines? What about the time you had six deadlines stacked and had to miss a few?

People have a tendency to judge themselves based on their intentions and how they perform the majority of the time. However, people will judge you based on your outcomes, and on how you perform in a choice few cases. If you are nice 90 percent of the time but you blow up at your team occasionally, then you're a mean boss, and that's how your team will see you. Likewise, if you double-check most of your work but sometimes let errors slip through, then you're error-prone.

You will be held to a much higher standard than your team members on every behavior you consider important. If you aren't demonstrating impeccable behavior, then your team will take that as a signal that they don't need to either. You must lead by example.

Something you will notice within the first year or two of managing people is that your team will reflect your behavior and your priorities. If you are always ready to accept new projects even if your plate is already full, your team will likely do that as well. If you are defensive of your time and priorities and make it difficult for others to impose, then your team will also reflect that.

This is largely a natural product of you being in a leadership role. Your team sees you as a successful example within the company or industry and will emulate some of the most striking aspects of your behavior. This may happen intentionally or inadvertently on their end, and not every person will reflect every behavior of yours, but it's an important thing to remember as you lead your team.

Examples

If you're going to fuss at your team for being late, you need to be at work on time or early.

If you want your team to be open and honest about mistakes, you must be open and honest.

If your team needs to stay late to finish projects, you need to do the same (or stay even later).

If you want your team to network and get involved in the community, you must also put yourself out there and participate.

The Risks

Many times this doesn't work as intended. Your team will notice some of your behaviors that you are blind to and emulate them as well. If you treat other teams with disrespect or condescension, then your team will do that. If you frequently get hung up on irrelevant details, your team will start to do that. There really is no way to avoid this completely because everyone has faults of which they are unaware, or strengths that can be twisted into faults when not used carefully.

For example, attention to detail is a very helpful skill and can make finished work sparkle, but it can cause you to spin your wheels on the finishing touches of a project that should have been finished days ago. Be aware of your weaknesses, because you will frequently see them pop up in your team.

Being able to be an effective coach for your team involves a lot of seeking knowledge about yourself and your own behavior. When you can do this, you will be better prepared to recognize problem behaviors and attitudes in your team and coach your team away from them.

Identifying Your Weak Spots

Because part of your job is to identify and correct weaknesses in others, you must first practice on yourself. This is a problem for most of us, because we aren't used to critiquing our own behavior. Regardless, it is a crucial step for an effective manager to take because of how it can improve your own coaching.

Ask yourself about situations that are stressful for you. For some of us, being in groups can be stressful. For others, it's public speaking, writing, defending an idea, or juggling multiple tasks. These situations will be where some of your weaknesses are most apparent.

How do you behave when in a stressful situation? Many of your behaviors to cope with stress will be reflections of your weaknesses. If you withdraw in order to finish work, that is probably a weakness. If you are quick to anger when challenged, that's definitely a weakness. Think deeply about your reactions to stress, and write down how you deal with it.

Another good exercise is to think about the one person you most admire. This could be a boss, coworker, public figure, or historical figure. Write down the top three things you most admire about that person. Perhaps they are very good at handling small tasks, or at making convincing arguments.

Those three things you wrote down are probably three areas you feel weak in.

Once you have identified your own weaknesses, you need to make a plan to correct them. Most weaknesses have both positive and negative sides, so the goal is not to scrub those characteristics entirely from your life. Instead, you need to train yourself to recognize that behavior when it is most negative, and overcome the habit.

Ask bosses, coworkers, friends, and your spouse to help you recognize your weaknesses by reminding you of your negative behavior in the moment. Since direct verbal challenges aren't always productive, pick a reminder that won't escalate the issue, such as a particular gesture they can make or word they can write.

When your team sees that you are recognizing your weakest areas and are working to fix them, you will have much more credibility when talking with them about their own weak areas.

A successful manager is one who can shape each member of their team into better teammates and workers. If you set an example by working on yourself, your team will see it and respond more positively when you coach them.

Embracing Differences

As a final point, don't expect your team to be you - part of their value is in the fact that they are different and have different approaches. Make sure you are careful in your coaching; if you coach them to reflect your behavior, make sure that specific behavior is actually necessary. If your only goal in setting an example is to make your team look and act just like you, it will not be successful. Remember, the primary goal here is to make sure your team members are effective, improving, and focused on the right things. You might have some helpful guidance to provide in getting them there. If you are unsure where your behavior falls relative to the line between improving them or getting them to act like you, just ask yourself whether it's self-focused or them-focused. Is your goal of enforcing a specific behavior to benefit them or to benefit you?

Chapter 4

Vision For The Team

Very little gets started or finished without motivation and direction. You may decide to start exercising more. Your reason for this may be that you want to get in better shape and feel healthier. You may want to finish a particular race. You may want to look better. You may love the experience of exercising with friends.

Your individual reason and motivation will have a big impact on what you're doing, how you're doing it, and whether you stick with it. Operating without direction is absolutely possible, and many people do just that, but it's very difficult to be successful if you haven't defined what success means to you. Having a clear direction and purpose makes it much easier to evaluate your progress and make adjustments in pursuit of a particular goal.

Likewise, one of the most important things you can do as a leader is to tell everyone where you're aiming. Not only do you have to make the direction clear for your own benefit, but you also need it for the team of people looking to you for leadership. People don't follow unless they want to go where they're being led or want to follow the person leading them there. As with working out, it is entirely possible for a team to operate without direction, but it makes it much more difficult to make progress anywhere if the members aren't all looking in the same direction. It is your responsibility as a leader and manager to make sure that you have a direction clearly identified, and that your team knows what it is.

Your team needs a goal, just like you need to set goals for yourself, and the company needs to set goals. Goals don't have to be high-minded and esoteric. The best goals are simple and achievable - cut routine processing time in half so that employees can spend more time on interesting and difficult cases, implement a new sales management process to raise sales by 30 percent, or even finish all work due to clients on time. Not every team has a "change the world" goal, and not every team needs one.

Thus, your direction needs to be calibrated to your team. A team capable of producing a world-class product and willing to put in the sacrifices to do so should absolutely have that as a goal. Anything less and it's likely your highest-caliber employees will go find a job offering that. But most teams aren't reaching for the stars, and this is a book about the real world. Most employees want a good, solid job with opportunity to grow. They're not trying to change the world, and they have more important priorities in their lives than making the company more money.

Far more important is what's in it for them. They probably won't care about making your company the market leader in widgets. They might care a little bit about the prestige that comes with working at a name their friends are familiar with. They might care about the promotions they may receive as the company grows. But they don't care about the company in and of itself.

So you need to make sure that when you set a direction and a goal, there is a clear reason why your team should want to get there. In general, most employees want to do a good job, be proud of their work, and to be recognized. There are an untold number of ways to set goals in order to facilitate this, depending on the needs of the company and your team. Some teams may want a goal of keeping quality extremely high or raising it to a new level. Other teams may want to build new processes or products to do their work better. There is no perfect goal, but you will be on the right track if it drives your team to do their best work and if it makes a clear distinction between success and failure.

The best goals are achievable and measurable. A nonspecific goal like "improve processing time" isn't good enough. Instead, try "finish building X improvement to decrease processing time," or "improve processing time by 30 percent."

Whatever you do, don't just pick a direction out of the blue one day and run with it as the new strategy; if you do, there's a high chance that you will end up not as committed to that direction as you first thought. Giving up on a direction is certainly necessary sometimes, but switching directions multiple times in a short period is a sure sign to your team that you don't know where you're going, and they don't have a reason to follow you there wholeheartedly. So be deliberate when choosing a direction to pursue, and consider potential choices for a while before rolling them out to the team.

On the other hand, you can't deliberate endlessly on different options and directions. Never making a decision is just as harmful as consistently revising a decision. The ideal is that you take time to choose a vision carefully, commit to it and make sure your team commits.

That last part is important: your team has to be as passionately sold on it as you are. It can be exhausting to be the only one pushing for something, so having your team on board is crucial to the long-term success of the vision. This means that you need to work to sell your team on the vision. The benefits will not always be self-evident to your team, so you have to illustrate those benefits for them. You are the ultimate owner of the vision, and a vision without followers is fruitless.

How To Sell Your Team On The Vision

As mentioned before, the first step is to make sure that your vision actually matters both in the grand scheme of the business and to each of your employees. It can and will matter in different ways to different groups, but it needs to have a natural hook for them. For example, the business may need a more efficient process to build widgets, but the hook for your talented employees who want more responsibility is that they now have a chance to design a process themselves. Don't expect that this natural hook will be self-evident to your team, though. You have to put in the work to sell them on it.

Again, it starts with understanding their plans and desires for their careers, or if they don't know what those are, then getting them excited about the big plans you have in store for them individually. You have a plan for how to give them more responsibility and improve their skills, so share it with them and get them involved in shaping it. Be honest about how you view the process, where you think the difficulties will lie, and what you think the benefits will be. One-on-one discussions are more persuasive than presentations to a group, primarily because large groups tend to muzzle or amplify dissent, depending on the makeup of the members, and fewer people ask questions in a large setting. One-on-one, most people will take a second and think of questions or give feedback.

Take feedback seriously. Your team will likely have some ideas of their own, and they could be really good. Don't reject their ideas simply because they didn't come directly from you. Seriously take their ideas under consideration, and decide if it makes sense to include them. This can be really difficult, especially after you've already put work into perfecting it, so many managers don't do it. Just remember that your team will be much more likely to buy into a vision they have helped shape.

Your Vision Versus The Company Vision

As you think about setting a vision and direction for the team, you should also consider the overall vision of the company. If it's not clear what that direction is, or if the company simply doesn't have one, you can still set goals for your team. More on that later. If your company already has a vision, you want to make sure that your goals align with the goals of the company, or at the very least don't conflict.

For example, if you work for a hotel chain and the chain's

vision is to be the luxury destination of choice for families, you probably don't want to make your team's vision all about doing things extremely efficiently to the extent that quality suffers. You might be successful within your team, but it's unlikely that you'll find much support from leadership because they will be focused on a very different goal of improving the member experience by over-delivering on quality.

Very often, however, a team's vision may be totally unrelated to the company's vision. An IT group in the same hotel company as the example above might have a team vision of using the latest and greatest technology to turn tasks around in less than 24 hours. This is probably unrelated to becoming a luxury hotel, and won't come into conflict. But this will also struggle to find enthusiastic support among leadership, because they are focused on something different: luxury experience.

The sweet spot exists where the team's vision accomplishes something important for your team and helps move the company in the direction it's already pointed. This ensures you have the full support of leadership, as your success will ultimately be their success. To beat the above example into the ground, if your IT team's vision is to use the latest and greatest technology to enhance the luxury feeling of the member experience, you will probably have quite a bit of support from leadership.

As a manager, it is your job to set a direction for your team, not your bosses. Your boss may have some ideas about what he or she would like to see out of your group, but the buck stops with you. This is a very important part of what you do, because it colors everything your team does. Choose your goals and direction carefully, and you will reap a motivated and well-directed team, as well as buy-in from your own managers.

If Your Company Doesn't Have A Vision

Not every company has a clear vision with which you can align your team. Some companies are so busy chasing various things that it's impossible to know which one of them is the most important. Some companies are so focused on what's happening right now that they haven't given serious thought to where they want to be in the future. Some companies have a clear vision spelled out but aren't actually doing anything about it.

This is a less than ideal situation to be in, but it's not impossible. Everything mentioned above about setting a vision for your team still holds true, and it's likely that you are already at least vaguely aware of what your team could be doing to advance their work and the company.

In these situations, you must find your own vision for your team and try to avoid an obvious conflict between your vision and the unclear vision for the company. It will at least give your team a solid direction.

Why It Matters

Having a clear and compelling vision is one of the most important things you can do for your team, but many teams either ignore the vision or don't take it seriously. This is not something you should emulate. Plenty of people make bad decisions and somehow come out fine on the other side, but you wouldn't extend it to recommend that people make those bad decisions. If your goal is to make your team the best in the organization, you need to show them where they need to be going and get their buy-in.

When you get it right, you'll find that your team will actually volunteer to take on significant parts of the load to get there. Your job morphs from having to pull the team along with you, to simply pointing them in a direction and letting them take care of things. This not only will give you more time to shape that direction, but it will also help your team grow as they identify the best ways to reach those goals and independently make plans to execute. Set a good vision for your team, and they will be the ones to improve their own skills and get things done.

Chapter 5

Prioritizing Work

One of your key functions as a boss is to help your team members make the most productive use of their time. To do this, you must understand which tasks are important, which are urgent, and which ones are neither.

I'm not the first to go over the difference between the important and the urgent, so I'll cover it briefly. While he was President, Dwight Eisenhower used a simple heuristic to determine where his time was best spent. He said "I have two kinds of problems, the urgent and the important. The urgent are not important, and the important are never urgent." In order to best use his time, each task was classified in terms of importance and urgency.

At the top of the list go the rare tasks that were **both urgent and important**. You often can't plan for these urgent and important tasks, and they naturally take top priority. For example, a major website outage would be very important and extremely urgent.

Next is the **important but not urgent**. These are the tasks that need dedicated time set aside to tackle, because they will never demand your immediate attention. Planning for future hiring needs is a great example of one of these tasks. It is important to prepare, but it can be very difficult to actually take the time to make a plan. If ignored, these tasks tend to suddenly become urgent too.

Next are the **urgent but not important**, which are exactly what they sound like. This is most of the noise that happens in your day and what causes most of your stress. With these tasks, always ask if they can be rescheduled, delegated, or completely ignored. Clients will often ask a simple question, but getting an answer would take hours of work. Most of the time, the question wasn't very important to the client in the first place, and you could have saved yourself hours of work by either saying no or asking deeper questions about their original question.

Finally, you have the **neither urgent nor important**. Don't do these. Work time is easy to fill with meaningless work, and being able to identify meaningless work is a valuable skill. For example, I have spent hours formatting a PowerPoint presentation, even though my changes would have no impact on how well the presentation went. Spend your time on other tasks instead.

As a leader, you need to spend as much of your time as possible on the important but not urgent tasks. Spending time here can often help reduce the amount of time you spend in the urgent and important category because you're taking care of the important tasks before they become urgent.

There is no foolproof method to decide which things are important and which are urgent - it all depends on where you work and your context. Cleaning the coffeepot is not important and not urgent for most employees at most offices, but it's definitely important if you work at a restaurant, and it could very well be urgent if the health inspector is walking through the door!

What To Do When You Have Too Much On Your Plate?

Unfortunately this is a frequent occurrence at many companies. Work has a way of expanding to fill the time allotted. If you find a more efficient way to complete a task, typically that means your "saved" time is now spent on another task. Some people view this as a curse, as if their main goal at work is to do nothing all day. This may influence some to underperform because, as they see it, the only reward for work well done is more work that will probably be harder. We'll assume that you do not fall into this camp, since you have already been promoted to a managerial position that likely required your boss to consider you a great asset to the team. But how do you make sure that you are focusing on the important things and letting the other items drop down the list?

The first and most important thing is to keep a list of everything that you have to do. This seems simple, but I see too many people who try to manage their workload primarily in their heads, and it leads them to focus on whichever task was most recently asked about or mentioned. Write your tasks down, and then you can take a high level view to rank your tasks in order of importance. I like doing this every day, but some prefer by week.

Now that you have a list of what you need to do and an understanding of which things are most important, there is still the problem of not having enough time to do everything well. You really have three options, none of which will be surprising, but all are useful at various times.

1. **Work longer.** This is the default option for many people, but it really should not be used except in extraordinary circumstances. A job that consistently requires overtime is a job that needs to be divided among multiple people. However, in some instances this is still the best option. Make sure when you choose this option that you are actually making an intentional choice and not just defaulting. Some days on a ship you have a storm and you need all hands on deck until it passes, but if you're constantly sailing through storms then you need to reevaluate your navigation.

2. **Spend less time on each task.** I think this is an underrated option if done judiciously. Some projects have an edifice of standards built around them that aren't necessary, and crunch time can be a good opportunity to reconsider how important those things are. This means doing each task less well and being okay with that. Many times this is

actually a good thing! If half the time you spend working on an internal presentation is polishing the details, then think about whether it's actually necessary or if it's just an excuse to avoid other work.

3. **Move the deadlines or cancel some work.** This is probably the ideal option, because it means you have to have an open conversation with your boss and other stakeholders during which everyone has to agree on what actually needs to be completed by a certain time. Usually this is not something that causes conflict, but it's important to make sure that everyone acknowledges 1) there's too much to do and 2) certain things are the most important.

Working longer, spending less time per task, and moving deadlines or canceling work all require very different skills. The first requires grit. Grit might be what got you promoted in the first place, since you're willing to do whatever it takes to meet the goal.

The second requires a sense of balance. Balance is really helpful in a small company in which there is always too much to do and the only hope of getting anything done lies in being sparing with your investment of time.

The third requires a grasp of strategy; you have to know how to decide when things can move or be canceled, get other stakeholders to agree to the change, and have the guts to actually cancel things.

Ultimately, all three are necessary skills of a great boss, and being deficient in a single one can cause an imbalance in your team. Understanding strategy and grit but missing balance means you will overwork and be prone to burning out. Balance and grit without strategy will result in the team getting high-quality work done, but always being distracted by less important tasks.

Make sure you are working to develop all three skills in

tandem, as each will serve you well.

Predicting How Long Work Will Take

In order to be able to prioritize tasks well, you need to be able to at least somewhat accurately predict how long a task will take. I think most people are intuitively able to do this, especially for smaller tasks and those tasks that have been done before, but you should keep two opposite ideas in mind when trying to estimate a timeline. First, big projects tend to take at least 50 percent longer than you expect. Second, work expands to fill the time allotted - if you give yourself two hours to write an email, then the email will be done in two hours.

As with most things, there must be a healthy balance between the two statements. Some people are overly aggressive in their timelines for open-ended projects and only account for the things they know will happen, even though every single large project carries with it plenty of unanticipated problems. Other times people are worried about overloading their plate so they assume that a relatively minor task will take more time than necessary. I've certainly been guilty of both.

This gets more difficult when trying to prioritize work for other people because their skill level and speed will be different from yours. You will need to be plugged into their work style to do this well.

For example, some employees will accept nearly any task and any timeline asked of them and will do whatever it takes to make it happen. On the face of it, that sounds like a great thing, but it quickly leads to their frustration, stress, and burnout. If you have an employee like this, you have to be careful what you're asking them to do and make sure that they are not silently overloaded. Check in with them to take their temperature on different tasks, and proactively ask if there is anything on their plate that they think should move to a later deadline or even be assigned to a different person. You ultimately want to train this person to learn to hit the brakes when there is not enough time to do the work asked.

Learning To Prioritize Work

Ultimately, this is not a complicated process. If you are able to communicate with your boss and other stakeholders, letting them know there's too much on your plate, then you can successfully prioritize all of the work you and your team have to do.

The most difficult thing for many people to do is realize the problem exists. The default reaction is often to just put our heads down and power through the tough time, but that's a sure way to burn yourself and your team out. Given that additional tasks are often relatively unimportant, that seems like a bad trade. Make sure that you are constantly watching your time and spending it in the best places. The higher you rise in your company and the more responsibility you have, the more demands will be made on your time and you will have fewer excuses to choose the unimportant things.

Chapter 6

Delegating Work

The hardest thing for a lot of new managers is to delegate work effectively and make sure it's done well, especially if they are managing in a field where much of the work requires skill and care. It's a difficult balance to strike between being a micromanager and being completely hands off, but learning this skill will be what allows you to truly be a leader of a highly effective team. In order to delegate work effectively, you need to find this balance.

What To Delegate

A lot of first-time managers have trouble determining what they need to delegate and what they need to keep doing themselves. This can lead to delegating very little work and even then only delegating the very easiest tasks. They tend to keep the more difficult tasks for themselves, since it takes a lot of time to train someone and it feels like it's faster to just power through it this one time (see below on how to get around this). Easy tasks are obvious candidates for delegation, but the real value in delegating comes with the complex tasks. If you can get your team to do the most difficult work and do it well, you will have dramatically increased the quality of your team as well as the amount of time you have to do other projects.

Like with everything else in teaching, you can't just hand off a pile of papers and tell someone to figure it out, at least not if you want them to understand it and be able to do it well. You have to first decide what they already do well, and then find the complex tasks you know they could do if you took time to teach them. Wait a little bit for the things that won't be as easy for them to grasp.

For example, a sales employee might be exceptional at crafting responses to tough questions, so all you need to do to delegate that type of task is explain the situation to them. That same employee may be very inattentive while contracting, so you probably don't want to immediately start giving them the difficult and important contracts to negotiate.

As this person improves, you will want to spend time with them during the tasks that they have more trouble with and give them one-on-one coaching on how to see those tasks in the same way that you do. You need to understand which tasks this person needs the most help with, which mainly requires paying attention. You know already who on your team is good at what and who is bad at what. Take this knowledge, look at the tasks you have to do, and begin to plan for how to show someone else how to do them.

In particular, find the hardest, most manual, worst tasks on your plate, and make a plan for delegating them. Most importantly, plan for how you're going to train people on them, and check their work. In many cases, training is as simple as showing someone how to do something once and checking their work. Other times it involves more skill training, so make sure you are working to build these skills in your team, with an eye toward the tasks you want these individuals to work on in the future.

Finding The Time

The paradox of delegating work is that you most need to do it when you have very little time, but doing it requires an investment of time. This means that most new managers feel like they don't have enough time to delegate and that it would be better to do the tasks themselves this last time. The trouble is, that scenario comes around again and again, and the situation hasn't changed. Realize that there will never be enough time when you need it most, and make a plan to start handing over the work well before it needs to be done. There are a lot of ways to do this, and certain methods work better for some people than for others. Some like to train over a period of weeks, while others would rather block off a large chunk of time and do it all at once.

It's easy to assume that when the time comes, you will have plenty of time in your schedule to train, but this assumption is frequently wrong. If you want the work off your plate (and you should) you need to take an hour to sit down and show the appropriate individuals how to do that work. Take another hour later that day or week to have them show you their work and process, and correct any errors. Finally, you'll need to look at their finished work independently to see if there is anything else they may have missed or you forgot to show them.

Building Trust

Many people become micromanagers because they don't trust anyone else to work to their standards. When you assign someone a task, you may feel the need to double-check that they're on track to complete it on time, that they're considering all of the different aspects, and that they're looking into the smallest details. These may sound like good things to a degree, but when done too often or too critically, they ultimately reflect a lack of trust on your part. When you begin as a manager, you have to start working to build that trust so that you can delegate work confidently to your team without fearing that they're making mistakes.

If someone already understands the task and how to complete it, have them check in with you once their work is finished and walk you through their process. Ask clarifying questions throughout to make sure you fully understand. The key thing to keep in mind here is "trust but verify." You are trusting them to do the work but verifying that it is done to the right standards.

If they don't already understand, then you do need to temporarily work closely with them to make sure they understand both the individual elements of the work they're doing and the broader context in which it's being done. To start, explain who they're sending it to, why it's important, how they'll use it, and anything else that can help give your team a reason to work on it other than simply "because the boss told me to." When talking about the individual work elements, it will depend on how established your team and processes are and how independent your people are. If you are walking them through a very well documented and established process, you may be able to quickly demonstrate the work and then leave them to try it alone, first consulting the documentation with any questions and then coming to you if it's still not clear.

If the process is more fluid and poorly documented, you're going to have to set some guardrails around it. Most likely, your process evolved over time from something simple and direct into a sprawling beast, and you were able to learn it over a period of months or years. Don't expect anyone else to absorb it immediately. You will need to start documenting it, which can either happen during the training or before, depending on who needs to write the documentation.

Correcting Work

As a manager, you have to be willing to tell someone to redo work that's not up to standard. This can be really hard for some people to do because most people dislike confrontation. It's hard on the person doing the correction, the person being corrected, and the relationship between them. However, no one does work perfectly every single time. Many times it will be "good enough," but sometimes it's an unacceptable level of quality.

Be careful how often you correct, and choose your instances of correction wisely based on how important the error actually is. These moments tend to be tense situations, which makes it really easy to damage a relationship by saying the wrong thing or even having the wrong body language. Additionally, people will look hard for ways to justify and defend their work, and they will know if redoing it is unnecessary. So be careful, because while this is a really effective way to get someone's attention and make them reevaluate their process, it can cause damage that is hard to undo. Make sure it's worth it.

When it is worth it, there are some things you can do to reduce the intensity of your feedback. Anyone who has been yelled at by their boss or experienced a time their boss seemed mad at them remembers it, so you want this to feel less like an attack and more like a chance to learn.

Point out the things that they need to reevaluate or redo. Be specific. If they failed to include an entire section of a document, make it clear that they need to go back and include that. If the problem is the tone of an email, tell them why that's an issue. You don't want to throw the work back in their face and tell them to redo it without making it clear what caught your eye. Give them a clear target to hit, and they will usually hit it. Asking them to figure out for themselves where the target is, after they've already tried and failed the first time, is likely to lead to another failure.

Also remember to praise them for the things they have done well in the process. This often gets overlooked, but it can help make it clear that you are not angry with them and that you are instead trying to help them do this particular thing better. It's very likely that there are things they have a solid grasp of and don't need your coaching on anymore, and you should recognize and acknowledge that improvement. People enjoy hearing that they're doing well at something.

When you are giving the feedback about what they need to do better, don't tell them every single step they need to take to finish the work. Instead, tell them what you expect from the final result. You want to develop their ability to independently figure out how to get there, and this means you need to show them the destination rather than the route. Newer and less-skilled employees will need a bit more coaching, and you should always be there to help reorient them if they get lost along the way, but the more you can develop problem-solving skills in your team, the less likely it will be that you need to spend your time guiding them.

You are coaching your team to improve, and sometimes that means you need to push them and make them redo work. If they never receive critical feedback, they won't recognize when their work isn't up to standards.

Remember The Why

Remember why you are delegating work. The obvious answer is because multiple people can get more done than a single person can, and this will clearly be key to your success as a manager. But don't discount the training aspect of delegating work. Many tasks may be tedious to you because you're fully versed in how to do them. Because you know so much about them and how many things can go wrong, you hesitate to have someone else do it because it'll just be faster for you to get it done. This is probably true in the short term, but this mentality cripples you in the long term.

A manager has to improve the skill set of their team, and must do this in part by giving them challenging work. Most likely, if you have the right team, they'll even find the challenge more interesting and less tedious than you do, because it's still a puzzle for them, rather than a repetitive task.

Keep an eye on the big picture here and the "why." Part of your job is to make sure things get done, and there are a lot of ways to do that. The default method a lot of new managers adopt is to try to do everything themselves, or at least to save the complicated parts for themselves. Some other new managers go to the opposite extreme and completely check out of the process, assuming that the person the work is assigned to will consider every angle and produce exceptional work.

Both approaches actually do have merit, depending on the circumstances, but your ultimate goal is to make sure that you are driving your team to individual and collective improvement. They should be able to look back every six months and be surprised at how much they've learned and what skills they've developed over that time. It's up to you to make sure that improvement is happening.

Chapter 7

Inheriting A Team

When you are first promoted to management, you will either build your own team, or you will be put in charge of an already existing team. Building a team from nothing is a challenge with many pitfalls (which we cover in detail elsewhere), but inheriting a team can lead to some especially difficult challenges for a brand-new manager to face.

If you are building a team from the ground up, everyone who joins the team has chosen to be there and is excited for the opportunity. This is not guaranteed when you inherit a team. Whether you are promoted to lead a team you were previously a member of, or are being brought in from outside to lead a team, there are issues that you should prepare for. Many issues will also require you to seek out and uncover them because they won't be brought to your attention directly.

In this chapter, we will primarily cover the process by which you pull your team together under your new leadership. Most new managers will have clear work-related goals they need to hit or processes they need to fix, and this chapter will not cover the relative merits of particular goals or the best bureaucratic process to implement them. My concern is organizing and inspiring your team to all push in the same direction in order to meet the goals.

As we've covered, one of the most important parts of leading a team is to point them in the right direction. Where many first-time managers fail is in making sure that the team is mentally ready to move in that direction. Key to this is to start building trust immediately and to ensure that you keep refilling the trust meter.

Your First Week As A Manager

One of the most important transformations that needs to take place for a new manager is the shift from doer to facilitator and coach.

You have just been announced as the new manager for this team, and you start your job on Monday morning. Likely you have had a chance to meet all of the team and are beginning to memorize everyone's names. Your first week will probably consist of significant amounts of learning, as you are taught company policy, company management process and procedures, the team's major processes and goals, and the company culture. It will feel overwhelming, especially since you probably just want to get back to work.

You have to resist the urge to dive straight in to doing work, as that's no longer your primary role. Instead, use this time to meet with the team frequently and in different contexts.

Meet with the group as a whole and introduce yourself, your goals, how you see yourself fitting into the group, and take any questions they have. Meet with each person individually for half an hour and come prepared with some questions to get to know them and their goals, and ask if there's anything you can do to help them. Meet with individuals to understand the details of major processes and the major pain points within. Most importantly, don't start trying to problem solve. Just listen, and try to understand. If you don't understand, ask questions.

If you see major weaknesses in a process, be careful how you bring them up. Most of the time, your team is already well aware of the weakness and has a reason for why it is the way it is. Part of your role will be to help the team determine ways to improve the process, but that part of the job does not start now. In the beginning, you are here to learn and understand.

Six Months

By this time, you should have a good working knowledge of

the company, your expectations as a manager, and most of the team's processes. Likely you have already started working to correct some issues.

Assuming you've spent enough time learning about the team's processes and most urgent issues, there is still risk involved with introducing changes. Primarily, you want your team to be a part of these changes and not feel as though the changes are being forced upon them. This means that 1) you need to have developed a baseline level of trust with your team so that they give you the benefit of the doubt, and 2) you need to heavily involve them in the process, being transparent about what needs to change and why.

Ask yourself the following questions to gauge where you stand with your team.

Big Questions

Does the team trust you and your judgement?

Trust is a tough thing to build and an easy thing to lose. A surefire way to lose the trust of your team is to demand that they trust you unconditionally.

Instead, a better way to gain trust is to first demonstrate trust in others. If you don't trust the judgment of your team, it's unlikely that they will place trust in your judgment. A mistake many first-time managers make is that they assume the best way to build the team's trust in their judgment is to judge everything.

I've certainly been guilty of this. I'll pass my opinion on something before they've had a chance to build or explain their own opinion. In most cases the right answer or path is relatively easy to find, so by inserting your opinion before theirs, you've made a big effort to show just how smart and capable you are, and you've excused them of the need to think critically.

Paradoxically, demonstrating that you trust someone else's opinion can improve the odds that they will extend the same trust to you. The best leaders know how and when to lead quietly and subtly. If your ultimate goal is to build your team members' trust in you, first start by showing your trust in them.

Does the team believe you are qualified, or does someone think they should have your job?

When someone thinks they deserve your job or that they are the real leader of the team, it puts you in a difficult situation. Many teams have individual members who play an outsized role, but it needs to be clear to everyone that you are the boss.

There are dozens of bad ways to do this, but the best way to handle this ultimately depends on the person you're working with and their ability to accept a different role than the one they've envisioned. If they will not accept you as a manager and refuse to help you settle into the role, you need to be firm and clear with them that they must make a change, either in attitude or in job altogether.

Many of you, especially for your first management position, will be understandably hesitant to threaten someone's job so quickly. Before you get to that point, you need to try multiple options to try to make the existing situation work. However, if someone on your team consistently has a bad attitude toward you and refuses to work constructively, you are limited to severe measures. A poisonous person on your team is not just bad for your and their morale; it also affects the entire team. You must work quickly and thoroughly to fix this problem, and your list of possible solutions has to include removing that person from your team.

Does the team think you don't understand what they do or why they do it that way?

This is a really easy one to solve. Learn their way of doing things and their system before implementing or even suggesting changes. Sit down and really try to understand why things are what they are, since even bad methods likely arise from good intentions. Understand that processes tend to evolve and mutate, and rarely are completely overhauled, so it's likely that some elements were grafted onto the process without a lot of thorough consideration and planning. Most teams learn to live with "good enough."

Because the process has evolved in this way, you are probably sitting with the person who has pushed that evolution. They will almost certainly have a personal stake in justifying their prior work and its current necessity. After all, it works today, so why spend valuable time fixing it?

A significant part of your job is to help guide your team through change. This may involve taking a tedious 30 minute process and reducing it to an automated 5 minute process. This will not happen unless your team wants it to happen. This will also not happen if you don't fully understand the needs, context, and flexibility of the current system, which you can only learn with time.

So take the time to learn; refrain from sharing your opinions or changes too early, and ask clarifying questions when you don't understand why something works a certain way.

Does the team fear a change in direction, real or imagined?

Most employees are afraid of the unknown when it comes to their day-to-day job. Change, especially when it's unclear and in the future, makes us uneasy. As a new manager, you will likely be responsible for implementing changes and improvements. The best way to bring your team along with you and make sure they aren't fighting the change is to get their input and make them feel included.

For example, if you are changing a sales script to better emphasize something in your product, reach out privately to people on your team to get feedback as you're putting it together. Give them a chance to be heard and make an impact. They will be much more likely to support the change in direction if it's partly their work.

One thing to be aware of, however, is that you can't ask for feedback and then ignore it if you disagree or end up pressed for time. That is probably worse than never asking for it at all. By asking for feedback, you are now responsible for making sure their feedback is taken seriously and improvements incorporated into the final piece of work. It is not necessary to use every suggestion from your team, but you do need to make a special effort to use their advice rather than check a box saying that you've asked for it.

Does your team miss the old boss?

In a lot of teams, it's natural to miss the former boss. It's likely that most of the members of the team had worked with them for years and have fond memories of their time together. This can cause some team members to compare every decision you make to what they think the old boss would have done, and this comparison rarely works out favorably if your team liked the former boss. You need to understand that this is a natural mourning period for the team, and there may not be a lot you can do to move it along. It will take people time to get over what they consider a loss.

The best thing for you to do is be a competent and compassionate leader, willing to acknowledge mistakes and ask for advice. If they are helping you adjust to the role, they will feel a sense of ownership and have a stake in making your tenure a success.

Don't try to be just like the former boss. As the new leader of the team, you are responsible for leading them and stamping your unique imprint on the team. This will be different than what the old boss did, in both approach and detail, but also make sure that it's not different simply for the sake of being different. Learn from what the former boss did successfully and the team enjoyed, and steal the techniques that worked. No matter what you do, the original boss will have had a deep and lasting impact on the team, so acknowledge that fact and move forward in the direction you think is best.

Is there a particular "problem child" on the team?

Some employees are just a pain to deal with. They never want to be a team player, they gossip and spread dissent, and generally are the 10 percent of people that take up 90 percent of your time. When hiring, you can generally screen these people out, but when you inherit a team you are often left with the team as-is, and rarely does it contain 100 percent team players.

So how do you deal with someone like this? First, after you've given the relationship a few months to settle, have a one-on-one conversation with this person, and simply ask them if this is the job they want to be doing. Problematic and destructive behavior is frequently indicative of dissatisfaction with the job, and sometimes a change is needed. If they answer that they don't want to be doing their job, you need to do what you can to help find them the right next role, whether that's inside the company or outside. While you may not get a straight answer right away, your open and genuine behavior in the meeting will encourage the other person to give you an honest answer.

Leading A Team Of Which You Were A Member Or Managing Someone Who Was Previously An Equal

Making the transition from a colleague to a boss is very difficult. It's not uncommon for some people to feel discouraged by your promotion, either because they feel they were more qualified or better suited for the position, or because they are worried that your promotion means fewer opportunities for them. Left unchecked, this can be a very poisonous atmosphere.

What you need to do as the new manager is sit down and have an honest conversation with your new team/former colleagues; talk about how this change impacts them, and give them a chance to ask questions. Ideally your boss would have done this before promoting you, but since management is the art of redundancy, it's better to do it twice and be sure it got done than to risk leaving it undone.

During this conversation, there may be questions that you are unable to answer immediately or things you haven't considered. Be honest about these things, and be open to following up and finding a solution.

Someone who was previously considered a candidate for your position is likely a valuable and productive employee, so you shouldn't have trouble getting your bosses to seriously consider the best options for them. Ultimately, you need to be working for this person to find the best possible spot for them, making sure they are part of this process. You can't impose a solution on them or do nothing, so listen to their concerns and take them seriously. This will go a long way toward building trust, and making this person your ally. As a manager, this probably describes half of the important aspects of your job, making allies instead of enemies.

Leading A Team As An Outside Hire

When you're new to the company as well as the team, there are a few extra things to work on to make sure the transition goes as well as possible. Not only do you need to build trust and communication in your team, but you also need to explore the existing links between your team and the rest of the company. It helps tremendously to understand the context in which the team works and how other groups rely on your team. This often comes naturally to someone who has been part of the company for several years, but you will have to be deliberate about seeking it out. Do not expect it to find you, because most other teams are worried about themselves rather than you.

In your conversations with your boss and your team, try to sketch out how your team interacts with others within the company. Get to know the primary contacts on those teams. Taking them out to lunch or coffee is a great option, but even stopping by their desk to chat a few times can be really beneficial. Your extra burden as an outside hire is to learn more about how things work in the company and who needs whom for what tasks.

Chapter 8

Building A Team

In some cases, your first experience as a manager will be while you hire and build a team instead of taking over an existing team. Ultimately, this requires a very similar set of skills to inheriting a team, but with a greater emphasis on different ones.

For example, instead of spending time understanding the existing culture and interpersonal workings of the team, you will need to spend time creating the culture from scratch. Likewise, there will not already be a process by which work gets done, so you will need to establish a process and standards.

Starting a team from nothing is extremely exciting because you get to dream big and design everything. It is also extremely terrifying, because you have to design everything. Like with any new project, building a team rewards care and diligence at the beginning of the process and requires flexibility every step of the way. Many people run into trouble attempting to design a system to perfection and get frustrated when the results don't match the sketches. Understand that this will happen and accept it.

As Mike Tyson once said, "Everybody has a plan until they get punched in the mouth."

Establish Work Processes

Surprisingly, your first experience building a team will probably be a solitary one. Your first priority is to figure out how to do the work that is already on your plate, and eventually to set up processes to allow you and future employees to do it well and quickly. As much as you can, set up the work in a way that is consistent and repeatable, creating a system that is easy to teach to others. Frequently reevaluate the way you work to see if there are things that could be done differently or better.

What you ultimately want is a process that is easy to teach, easy to monitor, and easy to do. If you can hit all three of those, then you'll be set up well to pass the work off to someone else as the team grows.

Your First Hire

As with a lot of things in life, the first move you make is extremely important. It's no different for hiring. Not only are you looking for a person to do a job, but you're also looking for someone to be your second in command. They will have a tremendous impact on how the team develops because they will out of necessity take ownership of a lot. They will be your sounding board for new ideas or processes, they will be the one who gives you the feedback as to whether your plans are workable and will probably contribute ideas of their own. It's important to make sure that you're aware of the role your first employee will have, and hire someone who can fit that role. Despite the fact that you just landed in this role, you need to start looking for your replacement, because it opens your future options up tremendously if you can take on a broader role, too, without the team struggling in your absence. So make sure that you are looking for a person who wants that growth and responsibility, and treat them as your right hand person when they come on board.

This means spending extra time with them. Not only should you show them how to do the work, but also how you think about it. Remember, you want this person to replace you, and the actual work is only part of what you do. You make decisions, so you need to show them how you make those decisions and the best ways to do so. Make sure you include them in your decision-making process, or at least discuss it with them later. Give them the leeway to make some decisions themselves, for the work that they own, and walk through the thought process with them.

Planning For Team Needs

It's also important to make sure that you are planning for the future needs of the team. Figuring out what your first hire will do is relatively easy - they generally help you do the things that you can't do in 40 hours a week. Once you start expanding beyond that, you start to have more possibilities for what each person can do.

Certainly, many teams grow by adding people who will do exactly the same type of work that everyone else does, but you should make sure you consider the possibility of increased specialization. Is there a part of the job that takes an especially long time to do or to learn, and are there two or more of those types of tasks? Think hard about assigning one of those tasks to a role that is primarily focused on that particular task. If you do this, your team will have more time to spend improving how the task is done. Even if none of the tasks on your team are big enough to justify a focused role, your team will benefit from having a particular person own certain repetitive or frequent tasks.

This type of task ownership occurs naturally in most teams and will happen in yours, but just because it will happen naturally doesn't mean that your team wouldn't benefit from preemptive planning on your part.

Youth Versus Experience

When filling out the team, you will have to decide how much experience those new employees need to have. On a general level, the tradeoff is time versus money. If you decide to hire someone earlier in their career, they will be less expensive to hire but will require a lot of your time to train them, as well as a longer ramp-up time to do their new job well.

Conversely, a more experienced hire will likely be able to start being productive very quickly but will cost you more money and will want more responsibility.

Many people or companies naturally gravitate toward hiring one or the other, but this is another decision that you will need to make carefully. Many roles can take someone who will grow into them, but you may not be able to afford to wait for that growth.

Creating A Culture

This is maybe the most important thing you can do for your team. No matter what you do, your team will have a culture and it will be largely a reflection of you and the values you demonstrate daily. As such, you need to be intentional about what that culture is and make sure that it's something you want.

Different cultures can work for different teams - some teams really enjoy the work hard play hard style, but the downside is that you may primarily attract young people prone to burnout. Other teams enjoy a relaxed low pressure environment, but you may run into complacency and lack of urgency. Some teams are full of practical jokers, others are completely buttoned up and professional.

The choices you make about the culture will have a big impact on who you hire, as culture is a major factor potential hires will take into consideration. It's important that the culture not be forced and that it's consistent. If you want your team culture to be fun and loose, for example, you have to be fun and loose and make sure you are taking the team to events that continue to build that culture.

After A Few Years

If you have been successful in designing and building your team, you will eventually have a number of very bright employees working with you. By this point, most of them will be fully trained and ready to take on additional responsibilities. Your job is to let them.

This sounds really easy, since all you have to do is do nothing.

But I can speak from experience that it can be really difficult to see a project that you designed and built taken over by someone else. Yet, nothing will make your team better more quickly than letting them tinker with the engine. You must help and guide them along this path, since you will often have a perspective that they do not, but you must also acknowledge that they have a perspective that you don't have, and they may be able to improve on your work.

It's really important to let your team know they have permission to change the way things are done. Your team will likely be closer to the actual work and be able to see many of the advantages and disadvantages of the way things are currently done. If they come to you with a good idea and a plan to implement it, let them know that they have permission to make the change. If you're someone who built the process, this seems obvious. A lot of your success probably came from assuming that you had permission to change the system. It's easy to assume that others working for you will share that same assertiveness. But they will not. In many cases, you need to encourage them to take that initiative, or they will allow the status quo to remain.

Remember, your job is to build your team into autonomous leaders, not mindless cogs in a machine. Part of that task is to build in the team a desire for improvement and a willingness to make things happen. Some people have this naturally, but if they don't, it can be taught. If you can teach this skill to your team, you will be a significantly more effective and creative team than almost any other in your company.

As the chapter of this title noted, you are trying to build a team. This is not the same as acquiring a team. Building a house isn't done when you acquire the materials. You have to shape those materials according to a plan in order to put them to a more effective use together than they could ever be separately. This is your mission as a manager.

Chapter 9

Career Shaping And Teaching Skills

For your team to get better, you have to teach them to get better. Each individual member of your team will not come fully formed and will never be fully formed. Part of what's so exciting about being a manager and so important about managing with love, is that you get to see your team develop new skills and improve in ways they hadn't considered. One of your most important roles is as a coach and trainer, so you must help them identify their gaps and begin to round out their skill set.

If you do this well, your team will be full of new ideas, innovative approaches to problems, and enthusiasm for exciting things they're working on. People love getting better at things they care about and demonstrating tangible progress. As their manager, you need to find what they care about, match them with what the team needs, and find a way to make sure they learn them.

You need to understand what it is that motivates your employees and where they want their careers to go in the future. For some people, you can just ask them and they'll tell you exactly what they want to do. These people are rare. Most others have a vague idea at best, and younger employees frequently haven't had the experience to know what they want to be doing in the future. Part of what you need to do is use your experience to help guide them along a path and try different things.

Determining Interests

If you're fortunate enough to have employees who have a clear view of what skills they want to improve and a plan to get there, then this section may be unnecessary. In most teams, however, the majority of employees are not like this. You already know what your team does on a day-to-day basis, the skills they currently have and their relative expertise at them, and their major skill gaps. What you need to do is figure out what parts of their job they really enjoy.

One simple way to find out is to observe the work they are especially diligent about doing well. If you always see high quality work on a particular task, then it's probably something they enjoy. To illustrate this, consider your own behavior. What are the tasks that you consistently do well and care about? Most likely, they are not things that you hate doing or continually procrastinate over. It may even be a task that you grew to enjoy doing as you got better at it, since it's human nature to enjoy the feeling of mastery. Watch your team for the things they are doing well and remember those things.

Also consider what aspects of their job they volunteer for and take initiative to improve. In these cases, your team is almost literally telling you what they enjoy and want to get better at, but managers often fail to notice. Keep an eye on the skills that your team has already independently been improving because you may be able to help them develop further.

If there are processes that they have volunteered or taken independent initiative to improve, then something about that process very likely appeals to them. Some people like better organization, others enjoy technical challenge, some simply like implementing change. Notice those behaviors in your team, and keep them in mind.

Finally, and most helpfully, ask them to tell you what they like and dislike. People are almost always forthcoming about the things they don't enjoy doing, and sometimes this process of elimination can reveal the things they do enjoy.

Some helpful ways to do this:

- Ask which tasks give them energy throughout the day, and which tasks drain their energy.

- Ask what they would personally fix in the company or department if they had a full month set aside to work on it.
- Ask for their most frustrating moment at work from the past twelve months.

Career Shaping

By far the best way to help an employee shape their career is for them to lead the discussion. There are many suggestions for how to have this conversation, but an extremely productive one I have collected and adapted from many people smarter than me is what I call Career Shaping. Many of these ideas are adapted from the Career Conversations framework in Kim Scott's book "Radical Candor," and I'd encourage you to read that for a different perspective on the process.

Career Shaping involves your employee telling you 1) what intrinsically motivates them, 2) their long-term goals, and 3) their near-term plan for moving toward those goals. Your role as a manager is largely confined to setting up the meetings and asking clarifying questions about what they're telling you.

Of course, those three ideas are not new. The problem is in getting useful answers that are meaningful to the employee and not just a check-the-box exercise. So much time is wasted by both employees and managers in filling out yet another career guidance document. To avoid this, Career Shaping is optional, requires weeks of preparation by the employee, and results in three to five concrete steps that the employee will take over the next twelve months.

The first and most important part is to get their buy-in. When you ask directly whether they want to do this exercise, most employees will say yes because you're their manager. Rather than an out of the blue approach, I like to wait until the career direction conversation naturally happens. If you're having routine one-on-one meetings (see chapter 13), this may happen as frequently as every few weeks, or as infrequently as once or twice per year.

During this conversation I'll bring up the idea of helping them shape their career, and explain the process to them. Due to the time investment, not everyone will want to go through the process, but most are already interested.

Career Shaping involves three separate hour-long discussions. To give the employee time to think and prepare, the first discussion takes place at least two weeks after they agree to participate. The two discussion after that also take place at least two weeks after the preceding one, so this entire process will take at least six weeks from the time it's first introduced. When these meetings are scheduled, it's best to include a short prompt in the invite that serves as a guide for the meeting.

- **The first discussion**: Share the story of your life and career, focusing in particular on changes you made, and why you made them.
- **The second discussion**: Your life could take many different paths. Think through a few of the most appealing ones and share what each different career peak would look like.
- **The third and final discussion**: What can you do in the next twelve months to get closer to achieving that peak?

That's the entire process.

Let's focus on each discussion in more detail.

The Past

The first discussion is focused on exploring motivations as illustrated by past behavior. Rather than ask about motivations directly, I ask for examples in their past of times they were dissatisfied with something and made a change. For each of those examples, I ask them to explain to me what that showed them about their motivations.

Everyone has different motivators in their life, and this meeting will help to uncover what those are. Many people have an idea of their motivators, but most of them have a hard time expressing it in a way that helps you fully understand. For example, someone telling you that they want to make a lot of money isn't as impactful as them telling you their story of growing up in a family that struggled, and sharing that the main reason they chose their major in college was because they wanted to get rich. Your goal is to help uncover those stories.

Your role in this meeting is to make sure you fully understand their motivations. This means you may need to ask clarifying questions about events in their lives, or deeply discuss the complexities surrounding certain decisions.

By the end of the meeting, you should have at least three to five major motivating factors in their life. Keep these, as you will use them in the final discussion.

You should close the meeting by thanking them for participating and sharing, explaining the prompt for the next meeting, and setting the date for the next meeting. The next meeting should be at least two weeks away in order to give them time to reflect and prepare.

The Future

The second discussion is focused on the distant future. I ask them to consider all the different paths their careers could take, many of which will be inconsistent with each other. For each of those paths, they tell me about the peak of their career and what it looks like.

The goal is not to define a specific career path, but to find the type of path they want to travel. Some employees want a career that gives them space for a non-career hobby like gardening, some want to be widely known as an expert in their field, and some want to build companies. By exploring many specific iterations of their ideal career, you can begin to find the connecting threads that better define their goals. Most of us know that our eventual career will look different than what we could think of today, but we can identify what type of career we think would meet our goals and make us happy.

This discussion involves sharing more nebulous ideas than the previous one, so back-and-forth questioning is necessary to ensure that you fully understand what about that career appeals to them. For example, if in one peak they are the famous CEO of a Fortune 500 company, they may be primarily interested in the fame, the money, the respect of their peers, the satisfaction of having built something, or helping push forward the progress of humanity, just to name a few possibilities. Each of those could be fulfilled in another career, but the careers that appeal to someone seeking fame will be very different than the careers that appeal to someone seeking to push forward the progress of humanity.

By the end of the meeting, you should be able to identify some common aspects of the different peaks they've spelled out. The goal of this process is not to come away with a defined map of their career, but a greater understanding of their idea of a successful career.

The Present

The third and final discussion is focused on the near future and setting specific goals. It's unlikely that your employee will reach the peak of their career in the next twelve months, so what can they do now to get them closer to achieving that peak?

The goal of this meeting is to finalize a plan for their next twelve months. This plan should be the employees to build and implement, not yours. You can and should help them plan, open doors of opportunity, and point them to things that you think will fit their interest, but the ultimate responsibility for taking action lies with them. You can help by offering to include this person in more external meetings, have them begin training new employees, or take a leadership position in a local professional group.

The best goals are concrete and specific. "Learn public speaking" is an admirable goal, but not one that is likely to be achieved. "Lead at least one talk in front of an audience of 20 or more people" is a much better one, because it is very specific, and specific goals are easier to make progress on. The next step is almost always clear, because it's extremely clear when the goal will be met. The less specific a goal, the harder it is to make progress and to know when it's complete.

The goals should be theirs, but you can help shape them into more concrete and achievable forms. This is where your notes from the first two meetings come in handy. Share what you learned about their motivating factors (from discussion 1) and their goals (from discussion 2), and make sure the goals are a good fit with both.

A great plan should generally contain three to five specific goals that they have a plan for achieving. Many motivated employees want to set a lot of goals, but they should set no more than five as their top priorities. Any more, and they run the risk of diluting their focus and doing none of their goals well.

Make sure that what you discuss is actually documented and shared between both of you. An email from your employee to you summarizing the goals usually works best. Some people find work or task tracking software very useful for measuring progress. Use these if they are helpful for them.

After the plan is finished, you should set up a follow-up meeting to check in on their progress. Every three to six months is more than enough. It is completely normal for them to change some of their goals over time. You need to make sure that these changes don't slow progress, but that the new goal is clearly defined and a path to completion found.

Meeting Tips

These meetings can take a wide variety of forms and the discussions can be very wide-ranging, so here are some tips to help keep the meeting as focused and productive as possible.

When these meetings are scheduled, it's best to include a short prompt in the invite that serves as a guide for the meeting. These meetings typically start by repeating the prompt and then letting your employee begin sharing. Most people find it easy to talk about themselves for an hour, so you will rarely need to encourage them to share more.

Don't be afraid to interrupt or to move away from a topic if it's been covered enough. An hour should be plenty of time for the discussion, but sometimes a conversation can get stuck and become unproductive, and it's your responsibility to get it unstuck.

Your role in these meetings is to make sure you fully understand what they mean. This means you may need to ask clarifying questions about events in their lives, or deeply discuss the complexities surrounding certain decisions or goals. It's their meeting, but you should still be talking or asking questions 10-20% of the time.

You should close each meeting by thanking them for participating and sharing, explaining the prompt for the next meeting, and setting the date for the next meeting. The next meeting should always be at least two weeks away in order to give them time to reflect and prepare.

Keeping The Plan Alive

Tracking career goals closely isn't always helpful. Because they are far away and never completely clear, defining and tracking the goal too rigidly can blind you to opportunities that would end up being a better fit. The best route to a distant goal is almost never a straight line. If you are tracking each individual step in relation to that goal and monitoring your progress closely, you will inevitably lose sight of that fact that a better route occasionally takes you in a direction that isn't directly closer to your goal.

As a manager, you want to listen for the places where you can help them fulfill their goals. If they eventually want to be in an executive position, start helping them get some of the experience they will need for that position. Let them define and run projects, introduce them to mentors, work with them on professionalism and long-term strategic thinking. Watch for skills they can improve and help them understand how to get better at those.

You won't be able to help with everything, and you need to be okay with that. If your employee ultimately wants to do something that isn't really related to what they're doing now, you may only be able to help indirectly. Here and there you might find projects that can help develop the skills they desire, but at the very least you can help encourage them in their goals.

If they have not imagined a career path yet, it's best to just offer the suggestion of what you've seen for their future career and let them think on it for a little while. If it truly grabs them, they will want to keep talking about it. As with skill development, you will not be able to lead this charge. They have to decide for themselves that it's something they want to pursue. At best, you can help show them the way, but they have to take the steps toward it.

If they seem uninterested about discussing their future, just bring it up periodically. Some people need time to decide that they want to plan their career, and as long as you let them know you are available to talk about it, you're doing your job.

Teaching Behavior

A lot of employees, especially younger ones, need some coaching in professional behavior. This is a really tricky thing to teach well because correct behavior depends on context. For example, some company cultures are very comfortable with cursing, and some are not at all. There is no one-size-fits-all model because each company culture is different. Despite the complexity, being able to identify and embody the right professional behavior is a crucial skill for your employees to have, and you need to help them build.

For example, even companies that are generally comfortable with cursing can have plenty of contexts where it's inappropriate. There may be other particular employees who aren't okay with it, meetings that require a more professional approach, calls with certain external vendors, etcetera. Most likely, the senior leaders who set the standard of allowing cursing are emotionally intelligent enough to understand the times when it is and is not appropriate. Younger employees in particular have a harder time figuring out where that line is.

More than anything, this is about watching for cases where your team isn't acting well and pulling them aside to correct the behavior. These are difficult conversations for you to have, as no one likes to be corrected about personal behavior. Make it clear that you are criticizing the behavior, not the person. Be merciful, especially at first. Learning requires failing, and while failing here can be especially painful to others in the room (I have vivid memories of cringing when I heard someone drop some R-rated vocabulary on a conservative mom of three), it's no less important or no less likely to happen. Understand that you had to learn the same things, and be gentle.

Teaching Skills

Teaching skills to your team members really requires three main things. You have to instruct, let them practice, and correct mistakes. Your team will never develop skills if you don't let them actively use those skills, and they will have a much harder time improving their skills if they aren't getting timely and helpful feedback. Teaching skills requires an investment of time on your part as a manager. You have to spend the time showing them how to do a task, but you also must spend time reviewing their work and fixing any gaps that remain. This can be really hard while you have many other things going on. Your time is limited, and this is one of the easiest things to put off until another time.

As I'm sure you realize, I'll be in favor of making sure you're taking the extra time to work with your team on training. It pays so many dividends in the long term. Not only are you helping build a team that can take significant work off of your own plate, but you are improving the career prospects of each member of your team. If you aren't improving your people as a manager, then you're just getting things done.

A Model Of Behavior

Since a lot of my work is in data, I frequently encounter extremely intelligent analysts who are really good at designing and following rules-based systems. They often got good grades in school because following rules works extremely well in that context.

One aspect of training I always have to emphasize with new analysts is that our pricing models are models of behavior. We've built them by looking at historical behavior, so they are generally good at predicting future behavior, but we have to be clear that it is only our best guess. The one thing that tells me I haven't trained an analyst well enough is when they defend poor analysis by saying their answer "is what the data/model said." The model might be a good guess, but it's not always representative of actual behavior.

I think about rules in the same way. Good rules are designed such that following them will lead to success. In school, some of the rules are showing up on time, not interrupting or disrespecting the teacher, and not getting into fights. They are in essence a model of ideal human behavior. If you do X and avoid doing Y, you will be successful. And generally, that's correct! That's a big part of why most of the successful students in high school and college are the "good kids" and rule-followers. They're following a model of human success.

But models are not representative of all successful behavior; they merely provide a decent simulation. It's important to recognize the model as a simulation, so you can break the rules when appropriate. Some rules need to be broken more than others. Some rules are almost flawless (mandatory school attendance - you can't learn if you're not there). However, others need to be scrapped entirely (any rule that exists but is rarely enforced). As simulations, these models are guides to be followed, not obeyed.

It's important not to equate rules with virtue. When you set up rules, you are attempting to set up guide rails for your team to follow to keep them on a path to success. If your rules aren't doing this, or are on the books without being enforced, they probably aren't worth having.

Chapter 10

The Hiring Process

If it feels like every chapter so far in this book is about something important, then congratulations! You've been paying attention. This chapter will be no different.

Who you hire matters tremendously.

A manager is only as good as the team they surround themselves with. Being a manager means that a significant portion of your time will be spent on activities not directly related to the work product. If you are a sales manager, a lot of your time will be spent not selling. If you're an IT manager, you will not spend much time coding. That work still needs to be done, but now the team can no longer count on your hands for the bulk of the work.

At some point, you will have the chance to build your team up with new members. This is your chance to not only grow the headcount of your team but also to grow the capabilities of your team by an even greater percentage. A great single employee added to a team should be able to add more than just the 40 hours per week of production that you could get from a normal employee. They should be opening up new avenues and capabilities for your team that make you much more productive. Sometimes this takes the role of bringing that capability themselves, and sometimes this means taking on well-understood tasks so that a more senior employee can focus on those new avenues. Either way, finding the right person for your team is absolutely critical.

If you know me, you'll know that I'm a big fan of college football. The passion, the history, and the strategy all appeal deeply to me. Because I'm pathologically unable to enjoy something without trying to find the metaphor within, I find myself thinking about comparing the challenges facing a college football team to those facing a team within a company.

The football team must attract and recruit the most talented players to their teams, and then they must also do a good job of developing and keeping those players once they're on the team. Some teams are able to be successful despite major failures in one of these areas. Some teams can coach anyone into a competent player, regardless of their potential. Some teams can simply wink and smile at a star recruit and get them to come play, even if they've never been able to train previous ones well.

What I want to draw your attention to are the teams that consistently perform both tasks successfully - they are able to find the players who will best carry their system to success and train them into what their system needs. These aren't always the players who can run the fastest or throw the farthest, since raw talent can mean very different things depending on the system you're using. Some teams need giant, strong players to physically dominate the other team, while others need fast, agile players to cover more ground. Equally important, if not even more so, is whether the mental makeup of the player fits the team.

There is no single definition for talent or fit - even though you would generally prefer a highly intelligent or diligent worker, nothing is more important than fit. If they aren't willing or able to play the style you want your workers to play, then they can't be successful in that role. If you aren't able to find any candidates to fit your style, you should reconsider whether your style fits the talent available.

Running A Hiring Process

How on earth do you run a hiring process? Many larger organizations have entire departments dedicated to recruiting and interviewing. If you're a part of one of these organizations, then your burden of interviewing will probably be lighter. You may not need to write the job description, find the candidates, screen the resumes, or take care of any offer logistics like checking references. Your only role is to interview and choose. Don't assume that this means you're off the hook. There is still a lot that goes into this, and you have been left with the most difficult and most consequential part of the process.

If you are still responsible for the other parts of the hiring process, then you need to understand that this is a very time-consuming process to do correctly. Any shortcuts you take are very likely to cause you trouble and pain in the future because you are making it less likely that you find the right person to hire, convince them to join, and convince them to stay. Because this person is going to be a critical member of your team and you will invest a lot of time with them, you need to make the investment early on to ensure that you are making the right decision. That investment can only be paid with time.

Job Descriptions

Your first step when hiring a new person is to determine what it is that they'll do, how you want to describe it, and how much experience you need and are willing to pay for. This clearly differs for each role and company, but you know what a job description looks like. Include the job title, a description of the company, a description of the job, some required skills & qualifications, instructions on how to apply, and you're good.

If you aren't happy with getting it 80 percent good and want to improve it marginally, here are some other tips. Professionalism is good, but dry descriptions will attract dry candidates. Make the description speak to the type of personality you want to attract. If you want buttoned up and professional, write like that. If you need energy and enthusiasm, write like that. If your role is for a junior person, emphasize how much they will learn, with specifics. Write the job description that you would apply for.

For the document itself, make it look nice. Screen it for spelling and grammar errors. If you aren't good at this, ask someone who is.

Screening Resumes

If you've done your job well and promoted the job posting, you should have many applicants. Now you have to sort through them and pick a few to screen over the phone.

Why a phone screen? The phone screen is a short investment of time to save hours of your time and the applicant's time. Well-executed phone screens should reduce your candidate pool by 50 percent or more. Don't bring a person into the office for a short screening interview when you could do it over the phone. An in-person interview will eventually be necessary, but it should not be your first step.

Picking candidates to screen is relatively easy. Find the people who have a resume similar to what you're seeking. There are also two caveats that might help you find candidates in more interesting places. One, be open to candidates who pique your interest for reasons besides well-aligned skill sets. They may not have the perfect resume, but some other aspect might make up for it. Second, be aware of your own biases. People naturally like familiarity and choose things similar to those they've seen before. That means they will be prone to choosing resumes similar to their own and with similar backgrounds. This might result in good hires. But by being aware that good candidates might take a shape you're not familiar with, you can get a much stronger candidate pool and make an improved hire. Look closely at the people you are rejecting, and make sure you are truly rejecting them because they aren't qualified rather than biasing yourself based on a name, college, former job, or some other ultimately irrelevant factor.

Phone Screens

The phone screen has one purpose. Make sure that your candidate is as qualified as they sound on their resume and that they are someone you want to bring in for an in-person interview. During a phone screen you want to have a short list of questions that you ask to all candidates, and you want to keep it to less than 30 minutes.

After you're done with all of the phone screens, you will probably have three distinct groups of candidates: the ones who clearly stand out from the rest, the ones who are clearly unqualified for the position, and the ones who could be good fits but are unexciting. I advocate only calling people that you are excited about and stopping the process with anyone in the third group. The likelihood that you find the right employee in this group is extremely low compared to the first group, and keeping these people on the list is just wasting your and their time.

Call the people in your first group, and schedule some time for them to come into the office.

The Interview

During the interview process, you have three main goals:

- Evaluate whether the candidate is capable of doing the job they're applying for.
- Evaluate whether the candidate shows the potential to grow into a larger role.
- Sell the candidate on the job.

All easy to say, hard to do.

How do you tell whether the candidate can actually do the job? There are dozens of books on the subject, and most of them do a very good job of explaining the process (My favorite is _Who_ by Geoff Smart and Randy Street). I can't improve much on their work, but I'll share some helpful tips.

Get the candidate to explain something they're excited about in detail. You're looking to see their process of thinking through a project. If they landed a big sale, ask them what the single most effective line in their pitch was. Why was it effective? Are there some that are less effective? Does it change depending on the audience?

By asking follow-up questions and digging deeper, you will quickly see who the top candidates are. Great candidates will have an answer for any reasonable questions because they've already done the work to think through what you may ask. A poor candidate generally does not have the ability to dig deeper into those questions. As you ask deeper questions, they will give shorter and shorter answers. The top candidate will frequently give longer answers.

Technical Fit

Do they have (or can they learn in less than six months) the basic skills necessary for success in the job? This is the most dependent on the specific role. These are table stakes in the interview process, and anyone who fails this test should not be in the interview.

Probe deeply to understand their experience with the technical skills you consider most important. If you're hiring for a sales role and they have years of sales experience, ask them to describe some experiences they've had. As they give details, continue probing and asking deeper and deeper questions. What I've found is that the candidates who are able to answer these deeper questions without stress can do it because they've already thought about it and evaluated their performance. As much as anything, this self-reflection can help predict continued improvement.

Team Fit

Will this person fit your vision of the team and will they be accepted by the rest of the team? This is pretty basic - does your existing team like this individual and are they willing to work with them?

Be extremely aware of potential red flags here. It takes a lot of time and effort to build a team that can work well together, but that can be destroyed quickly by the wrong person. If someone is a great technical fit but a terrible team fit, they are not the right person to hire.

Culture Fit

Does this person's standards, morals, and vision fit with the company? For example, if your company has a strong culture of gratitude, where no good deed goes un-thanked, you will need to heavily consider whether this person you're interviewing would work well in that setting. An egotistical person may not be able or willing to bend to reflect the company's standard in this area. Nine times out of ten, a person who raises red flags on this portion of the interview decision will not be an overall asset to the organization. They might be a "productive" employee, but they will be the source of many headaches and strife. These types of employees are often the hardest to manage, because there's an unbridgeable disconnect between what they and the company think are important.

Feedback And Review

After the interview, and before talking with anyone else, each interviewer will sit down and write out their thoughts on the candidate, often following a scorecard that we've put together for the role and responding to specific questions we're asking about their opinion. If you ask for general thoughts, you get a general (i.e., unhelpful) answer. Specific questions typically draw out better responses.

After your team has finished writing down their opinion of the candidate, conduct one-on-one reviews with everyone who talked to the candidate, but avoid asking the group as a whole for their opinion. Group reviews tend to be dominated by one or two voices, and the opinion of the vocal few can quickly become the entire room's opinion. Typically these reviews can be taken care of in less than 5 minutes by asking "What did you think?" and "Were there any red flags that would cause you not to hire them?" Refrain from sharing your opinion yet, as that may influence the feedback others give you.

Only after the scorecards and one-on-one meetings are finished should you convene the larger group to discuss. Now that you've made sure each person has carefully considered their opinion, the discussion tends to be more productive with more valuable insight.

The most valuable feedback at this point is anything that disagrees with the opinion you've already formed. If your opinion can't hold up to the points that others bring up, then you've saved yourself a lot of trouble. And if it can hold up, you will need to articulate a good defense for why those points don't matter or you think they can be overcome.

Also review your interview technique. What worked? Did your questions result in the answers you needed? It's very helpful to do this with someone else who was in the room, since you can add their insight to yours. This is less to help you evaluate the candidate, and more to ensure that future interviews will improve. Ask the other person what parts of the interview were successful, and which were less successful. Can they give you any feedback about technique?

Making The Hiring Decision

What happens if you're not sure about the candidate after the interview? It's very common to walk out of an interview feeling ambivalent about a candidate. They didn't disqualify themselves, but they also didn't inspire you.

Reject every one of those candidates. They will not be your

best hires, and you are settling by bringing them on.

How do you know when you've found the right candidate? The top candidates will have you skipping out of the room, excited about the possibilities.

What if I don't find the right candidate? You owe it to yourself to keep looking for them. Don't compromise on an ok candidate. You will be investing significant amounts of your time and energy into this person. Why choose second best? You may need to review your salary and requirements to make sure they're consistent with the market, but once you're confident in those, don't settle.

One of your most valuable assets is your time. If you make the call to invest significant amounts of time into training a subpar hire, it will reflect poorly on you. Spend time on hiring the right person, and you will be rewarded with a hire who saves you time and headaches, and ultimately makes you look really good. It's one of the best investments you can make as a manager.

Convincing The Candidate

Of all the parts of hiring, this is the one that I see emphasized least often. Yet, for the people you most want to hire, it's the secret weapon that can help you actually bring this person into your company. Top candidates are smart enough to hedge their bets and interview multiple places. Those people tend to outshine their competition, so they end up drawing a lot of offers. You need your company to be the one that sticks out to them.

When you've decided to make an offer to a candidate, your job is not finished. You have hooked the candidate, now you need to work to land them. But you may be wondering, after all, that they are the one trying to convince you to give them an offer, so shouldn't it stand to reason that they already want the job?

As with many things, this is theoretically true, but the real world tells a different story. Most likely, the candidate that you are hiring is one you are really excited to work with (if you aren't, why are you hiring them?) You're probably not the only one who is excited about this person. You need to make sure that the full package you're offering can beat out your competition and land this potential new employee.

Most of the time, you won't be able to offer the most attractive combination of salary, benefits. Even if you could offer the most money, you need to give them a compelling reason to choose you and your team. Most employees make their choice on emotional factors rather than cold financial logic. I doubt you would willingly work in a miserable job that came with a higher salary, and you shouldn't expect anyone you hire to either. You have to convince them that this job is one that they will enjoy doing and will help advance them toward their goals. If you can't, you won't be able to make many good hires and you won't be able to keep the good people you have hired.

Get them excited about the work they'll be doing. Working with you. Working with your company. Working with your team. This starts as soon as you post the job, and it continues through at least the first few weeks they're employed.

First and foremost, you have to be excited about the job and the opportunities it presents. If you think the job is thankless and menial drudgery, candidates will pick up on that and discount the opportunity accordingly. If you think the job is high-stress and painful, candidates will pick up on that as well. Who would want either of those? Focus on the benefits and advantages. The top candidate will understand the downsides to the job, so you don't need to add additional focus on them. You have to sell them on the upside. The top candidate is usually willing to put in hard work for long-term gain, so you need to focus on what that gain looks like.

When talking about the job, you need to be honest about the requirements and responsibilities, but that doesn't mean you have to paint things in a negative light. All challenges are opportunities in the right hands. Clearly, some parts of every job are just plain tedious, but if that's the light you paint your job in then you will never hire a great candidate. Equally important is to not oversell a job - smart and talented people will see right through you trying to describe a receptionist job as something more prestigious.

Ultimately, you need to highlight the positives of working in the role, especially considering what your ideal candidate would love about that role. Find those things, and hammer them home. If you need a bright, bubbly personality to charm guests, highlight the opportunity to be the first face of the company, never be bored, and be on your feet rather than behind a desk. If you need someone who enjoys coordinating 50 simultaneous incoming calls and visitors, highlight the logistical challenges they'll face and the fact that they're the hub of the company. Describe your ideal employee for the position, and write the job description as if it's a letter written directly to them.

Never mislead a candidate or be dishonest with them. That is a waste of time that will only lead to quick turnover and hurt feelings. If the job can be menial, then you need to say so. If it can be stressful, then they need to be aware. The difference is one of emphasis rather than of kind. Tell the truth, but express your genuine excitement for the position.

Entry Level Hires

For an entry-level candidate, talk about what they'll learn and the things they'll get to help build. The most promising entry-level people are ambitious, and you want to show them that your company is the best place for them to grow. Again, don't oversell a position because most entry-level employees simply aren't ready to handle running a large project solo, but ultimately you want to emphasize the opportunities available for someone who is willing to seize them. If you aren't able to envision a position where an entry-level employee would have those opportunities, then you need to reconsider whether it's possible to attract a great entry-level candidate.

Senior Level Hires

For a more senior person, having autonomy and ownership are very important, as well as a good company culture. By the time people have worked for a few years, most of them have been in at least one job where the culture was lacking, and the ones you want to hire will be making a decision at least in part based on how happy they will be spending their days in your office, which is largely a reflection of company culture. We discussed this more in chapter 8, but culture is not foosball tables and free cokes. Instead, it's a company clearly driven by a set of ideals and behaviors, like honesty, innovation, and customer service. It's the people and their behavior, not the decorations.

Tying Up The Loose Ends

It's important to remember the other candidates who were not a good fit. Too many companies, after they've rejected a candidate, never follow up with that person to let them know. Obviously that person will get the message after a few weeks without hearing back, but I think that's a really disrespectful way of handling things. You would rightly be miffed if you sent a candidate a job offer and they never acknowledged it, and I think the courtesy needs to extend the other direction.

After you've hired and locked down a candidate, make sure to call everyone you've had a phone screen or in-person interview with and let them know the decision. It's not a fun activity to deliver bad news, but it's very important that you take the time to treat others with respect and acknowledge the time they've given up for you. Don't burn bridges; some of these candidates may turn up again, but be clear that you have hired someone else for the current opening. Most people do not ask for an explanation, but if they do, try not to go into specific detail about their candidacy. Typically saying that another candidate was a better fit suffices.

Call everyone else and tell them the bad news. Don't email them. Don't ignore them.

Networking

All of the advice about hiring is irrelevant if you are not attracting the right candidates. Unfortunately, as much as we all think our companies are great and practically sell themselves, it's actually a rare thing for a great candidate to find you in a sea of other job postings. Many managers agonize about the right way to write a job description or the best ways to promote their job opening. As long as those are done competently, additional improvement pays off very little.

A better place to put your time and effort than in agonizing over the small details in the job description is in physically finding a network of people to contact. As anyone with significant hiring experience can tell you, most of the best hires come from personal recommendations rather than online applications. As a manager and now recruiter, you have to make sure you know enough of the right people to get these recommendations and let them know when you're looking for someone. Ask if they know anyone who would be a good fit, and return the favor when they ask you the same question. If you do this well, you will have far more great candidates than you do open positions.

Chapter 11

Accept Blame & Give Credit

Every one of us has been in a situation at work where something was sent to a client that shouldn't have been, somebody made a major mistake in analysis, or something happened causing the boss to look for someone to blame. Each of us has been the culprit in that situation and hopefully we've learned to handle it with grace.

Similarly, now that you're managing, there will be times when someone on your team is responsible. They put together the work that was incorrect or they made the ill-advised remark. Making mistakes is part of the learning process, so we know this will happen. But there is a big difference between understanding the abstract concept of "learning requires failing" and being able to handle a boss or client coming around looking for a scalp because of something your team did.

In these situations, it's usually the case that you weren't primarily at fault. In your view, you gave the employee clear directions, and they failed to follow them. When your boss comes looking for someone to blame, the first instinct is to point in the direction of the employee and watch the fireworks.

Of course, we're not literally pointing a finger and accusing someone else of making a mistake. Many people don't enjoy confrontation and will say a lot of things to wriggle out from under the microscope. This takes shape in more subtle ways. Do any of these sound familiar?

"The bill did not get sent out on time, but John is supposed to remind us to send them out three days before they're due. He didn't do that."

"We had a junior analyst produce that report, and they missed an excel formula."

"I told Jim about this deadline a week ago and how important it was, and he still missed it."

If you're doing this, stop. It is cowardly. In each of those cases, the blame you're assigning may be factually true, but the larger responsibility is with you. That's the burden of a manager - you're ultimately responsible for your employee's actions in those scenarios. If they missed a deadline, it's because you didn't check in. If they screwed up some analysis, it's because you didn't check it and discuss it with them. As soon as you accepted the job, you lost your ability to wash your hands of someone else's mistake and say you had nothing to do with it.

If you've ever shifted blame to an employee, hopefully you had a shrewd listener on the other end who didn't take the bait and instead held you to account for your employee's error. This means coming to you to handle the cleanup and to figure out the best way to train them to not make this mistake again.

Since you are already responsible for your team's mistakes, you need to accept the blame for things getting out of control and take ownership of the solution. Technically, you were not the one who caused the issue, but that's a bit like blaming a dog for having an accident inside when you didn't take them out all day long. You are the responsible party, and you need to act like it.

If you're not managing the work your team is doing, then why bother calling yourself a manager at all?

Accept Blame

You have to actually believe that you are responsible for your team's failings. Saying it seriously is better than saying it through gritted teeth (and saying it through gritted teeth is better than not saying it at all). If you internalize it and do accept blame for your mistakes, you will be much more effective.

As we've discussed, your goal as a manager is to help your employees become better. If they consistently make significant mistakes, then they or their superiors should be blaming you for the errors. If your team members are new and are doing tasks for the first time, then you probably should have checked their work more thoroughly. If they're just beginning to step out of your shadow and produce work that generally doesn't need to be checked, then you have made the mistake of not training them to either recognize their mistakes or ask questions. If they are still making the same errors no matter how much you help them, it's your fault for not moving them to work that's better suited to their skills. Recognize that in all of these cases, there is an intervention that you could have made, and if you had done it, the work would have been better.

This doesn't mean that you need to micromanage your employees and stand over their shoulders to ensure they never make any errors. Growth requires making mistakes, but growth can also be accelerated by a coach who can recognize errors and recommend fixes. If you want to be an effective coach for your team, you have to care about when they fail. This doesn't mean that you should get angry or emotional when your team makes a mistake. Instead, you should be invested to helping them overcome these mistakes and setting them up to succeed in the future. A manager is in a unique position to help coach their team, and a critical step to understanding the importance of that role is to acknowledge when you have failed as a coach.

So what happens when you master the art of taking blame? For one, you're likely to be more diligent about your employees' work, since it will directly reflect on you. If you see someone lacking in a skill or lazy about certain types of work, it suddenly becomes a lot more difficult to ignore because now you're under scrutiny for it. This means you have a bigger incentive to invest in actually improving how your employees work and their skills, or transferring or firing those who refuse to improve.

Taking the blame is ultimately about taking responsibility for your role as a manager and internalizing the fact that your relationship with your team has changed in multiple ways. You are the boss, and with the promotion, pay, and prestige comes a significant downside of always having to be the one holding the bag. It's a very rewarding role, and one that you can grow into, but only if you accept the role for what it is.

Giving Credit

The flip side of taking blame for all mistakes on your watch is that you need to give away the credit for every success. When your team does well, it is because of things that they have done well rather than anything you did. Without their effort and brainpower, it would not have gone as well as it did. Everyone loves to hear praise for work they have done. Some people have a hard time taking a compliment and will try to deflect praise, but they still need to hear praise for the work they're doing.

There are two main groups to give credit and thanks to: the Connection-Makers and the Detailers.

Thanking the Connection-Makers means handing out credit to the people who help manage your project, to those who clearly defined the scope of work, or who helped communicate with the client. This is common courtesy and gratitude, and you should be practicing it intentionally. If you have finished a project with a difficult client, thank the person who owns that relationship and knows how to make sure conversations don't go sideways. Without that person's smooth handling of the relationship, the entire project would have been significantly more difficult. At the very least, they are the ones on the front lines taking the first and most furious assaults and insulating you from a lot of the damage. That work takes skill and effort to do well, and they should be thanked anytime they help your team.

Thanking the Detailers means praising the people who did the details of the work and making sure their contributions are well known. If you're a manager, this means messaging the entire team after a successful project and specifically praising individual team members for their contribution. If your superiors are included on the email, it helps your employee build their career, since they're looking better in the eyes of higher-ups in the company.

I think most people think of themselves as belonging to one of these two groups and usually have a hard time recognizing the contributions of someone from the other group. It's very easy to dismiss someone's contribution as less significant when you aren't familiar with it. If someone "only talks to clients" or "makes a simple update to a website" it can be hard to recognize that the contribution takes as much skill and effort as yours. But you have to make sure you are recognizing everyone's role, and this becomes more important the higher up in the company you are. Praise from a CEO is always going to feel more important to a worker than praise from their direct manager, and a good CEO is liberal with their praise of the front-line workers and managers.

Make sure you are giving praise in more than one way. Verbal praise is obviously key, but it should not be your only way. Writing out an expression of your gratitude, in an email or a handwritten note, is a really good way to brighten up someone else's day. Think about your reaction when you received an earnest note of appreciation. You probably were proud of yourself and even showed it off to people close to you. As a manager, you are now in the position to do this for other people, and you have to make it happen.

Isn't it a bad career move not to take credit for your success?

In most cases, not being recognized will have a negative impact on your career. However, you do not have to actively seek and take credit to be recognized. The harder you pursue recognition, the less forthcoming it is. We all remember the person who wanted to shine the brightest and look the best, and most of us were annoyed at that person's hogging of the limelight.

You can pursue this path, and you may even get some benefit out of it, but it's a look and attitude that typically wears on people over time and especially on those closest to you. The same benefit will be there if you take a step back and praise others instead of yourself. The world has a way of rewarding those who build others up instead of building themselves up.

There are some things you can do to make your role in the overall success of the project and team members visible. Being involved in the process is obviously important, but helping to give guidance and feedback and redirecting effort when necessary are also ways to be involved.

Just remember that when people look back at all of the projects that have gone well, you want them to see a common denominator - you and your team.

Won't I get outshined?

If you want to succeed as a leader, it's a lot better to be seen as the head of a bunch of superstars than to be an individual superstar yourself. An obvious example is found in sports. Nick Saban is widely seen as the greatest college football coach in history, and a master tactician in his own right, but one of the first things you hear about the Alabama football organization is the coaching tree that he has built and is continuing to build.

In fact, he has been so successful at this that his assistant coaches keep getting hired into better jobs. This alone might be a problem, except that it leads to his reputation as a leader who will advance the careers of his subordinates, so he is constantly able to hire the best assistants.

Contrast that with LeBron James, widely acknowledged as the greatest current basketball player and the de facto coach and general manager of any team he plays on. LeBron is so skilled that he can almost single-handedly propel a team to victory over any opponent. Yet LeBron has only won the NBA Title three times, losing in the final round six times (as of February 2019).

A lot of this difference is natural to the sport, since it's easier for one basketball player to impact a team than it is for one football coach), but it's also instructive to consider how different LeBron is as a leader. He rarely plays with the best talent, nor does he appear interested in doing so.

Based on his career so far, it's easy to assume that LeBron is primarily concerned about being the leader and primary decision-maker of his team, and this attitude impacts the star players who join him. The role players who join him often exist as ancillaries to LeBron's greatness rather than supporting members.

Nick Saban will frequently have players and coaches praised more than he is (Kirby Smart, Lane Kiffin, Tua Tagovailoa). LeBron has never had a player or coach praised more than him. If you want to attract the best talent, be more like a Nick Saban, and less like a LeBron James.

As LeBron shows, it is possible to be the shining star and still be extremely successful. The problem is all of that success is on his shoulders. He doesn't get to take a day off. The team wins if he plays well and loses if he doesn't. If he wants to add to his legacy, it takes a superhuman effort on his part in addition to luck. But as Saban shows, having talented assistants around who can outshine you will often lead to the same results with less drama.

Chapter 12

Correcting Poor Performance

One of the most difficult transitions for some people is taking on responsibility for correcting bad behavior or poor performance. The first time you have to do this, you will probably default to the techniques that your boss used on you. If your boss yelled at you for messing up something important, then that's what you'll do, too. If your boss tried to give a pep talk, you will too. If your boss ignored problems, then there's a good chance that you'll undersell them as well.

You need to recognize that you will be prone to this behavior, and most likely that technique will be the first one you try. It will likely not be the one that you take naturally to, but it's the mask you've seen worn before so you will try it out.

No single method is necessarily better than others, and each method can be harmful in its own unique way. Yelling at people can cause them to resent you and shut down around you. Being relentlessly positive may blind you to obvious unsolvable problems. Ignoring problems will more often than not result in things getting worse rather than better.

You will develop your own style that works for you. But what you need to do is make sure that style does not cause harm to your team and instead effectively builds them into the productive employees you know they can be. As we've repeated time and time again, it's all about managing with love, approaching your corrections from a position of wanting to improve their skills rather than a position of anger or criticism.

This is not always how people approach it, and most likely you have your own experiences with a boss you thought was irrational and mean. You are now in their position, and the natural human state is to behave just like they did. Be intentional about behaving differently, and caring deeply about your team.

This will feel very uncomfortable at first. Most people either try to avoid conflict or try to win the conflict. You are trying to channel this natural emotion into a productive lesson for your team, and that will not feel natural to you. You will make mistakes. The key is to work at it until it feels more comfortable. Be open and honest about your struggles. You will say the wrong thing, come into a meeting angry about something unimportant, or feel the need to vent at someone who has done something wrong. Accept that this will happen, and commit to recognizing and fixing it when it does happen. We all have our weak days and episodes we'd like to take back, and all you can do is to make sure you are committing to continual improvement and not making the same mistakes over and over again.

When To Bring It Up

You will have an employee who is just not cutting it in one way or another. One of your responsibilities is to make sure that person knows that low work quality has been noticed and needs to be improved. This clear acknowledgment happens less often than you think - many managers (and I've certainly been guilty of this myself) will think that it's not worth the confrontation or that the employee already knows they screwed up. Actually talking directly to the person and saying the words out loud is important.

You don't need to criticize every single little thing, since that is a surefire way to foster resentment from your team and cause them to start second guessing their work. Don't make corrections publicly unless absolutely necessary. Praise publicly, criticize privately.

Focus on the important things, or the things that both you and your employee have agreed are important for them to work on. Are they late for a meeting once and seem embarrassed by it? Have mercy, and let it go. Are they consistently late for meetings? Take them aside privately and let them know that you have noticed and that they need to be there on time in the future. Unless very warranted, don't dwell on this - a quick 30 second conversation is more than enough. If they continue to be late, this is when you need to take them aside and have a more serious conversation. Try to hear their side to understand why they are late, but also be clear with them that they are not meeting the standard.

In practice, most employees get the message before you ever have to speak with them, and the vast majority of the rest do after the first conversation. You will have some employees who just can't seem to get the message and do not show improvement. You could ignore the problem, but you need to begin working with this person to find a way to reach them. If still no progress is being made, you may need to fire them.

How do you reach them and improve their behavior? Firstly, you need to find out about their motivations. Usually, both you and the individual genuinely want to see improvement in their work quality. However, if that motivation is not there for you or your employee, this becomes a much more difficult conversation.

Checking Whether The Motivation Is There

The obvious first step here is to directly ask your employee about their motivation and whether they want to be there. You can guess that most people will answer "yes" to these questions. They understand that answering "no" could mean losing their job, and most people do not want to court that prospect.

If they are bold enough to answer no, that they do not want to be there, then skip the next section and read how to handle unmotivated employees.

If, like most people, they answer yes, then you need to begin digging a little deeper to uncover what they are motivated by and what they want to be doing. You already know that they are not showing improvement, so that can be a good place to start.

Ask about the project that they are working on and why they seemingly haven't been trying to get better at it. It's extremely likely that you will learn something valuable here about the process, so don't try to make this an argument by defending or explaining. Simply listen without judgment, and make note of things that seem particularly important or might even help you improve how you manage.

Are they late for meetings because the meetings are always pointless? Do they dread working on this project because the manual tasks in it drain them of energy? These are things you hopefully would have uncovered or noticed a while ago and can confirm, but it's very helpful to hear it directly from the other person.

There may also be something going on in their personal life. Tread carefully here. This is not your space, and there will probably not be a lot that you can help with directly. Be supportive if asked, but don't insert yourself into their personal space. To the extent that you can, have mercy and give them working flexibility as they need it. If they want to talk about their troubles and share the details, let them. If they don't, then respect that decision too.

Regardless of the why, you still need to work on the motivation and make sure your team is doing their best work.

If They Are Motivated

Sometimes people just have a hard time grasping a concept or improving a skill. They really want to do it but are struggling for one reason or another. If both sides want this to happen, the way forward is not complicated. The two of you need to come up with a plan for them to get better and actually stick to it.

We've discussed this already in a previous chapter about career goals, but it bears repeating. Plans are almost always better when they come from them instead of you, because they will be much more likely to commit and stick to something of their own design. You should help provide guidance, and point out the areas where they're being overoptimistic or not challenging themselves enough. It may not be realistic to spend an hour every day working on one particular skill, or on the other end of the spectrum you may see them sandbagging and saying they will do 30 minutes a week when you know they need and can do more time.

Some skills take a lot of practice to master, so you want to make sure that they are getting the right kind of practice. They will need coaching on the right way to do the task, as well as coaching to correct their work. Many times, you will be the best person to do this training, but think hard about whether they would be best served by learning from someone else. This person may be on your team, in your company, or even outside of the organization. Some of these training options are easier to organize than others, but all should be open to consideration. Online classes and videos can be helpful but usually aren't sufficient on their own. Ask their opinion, and see if there's someone they know who would be willing to help teach them.

It's good to review progress periodically, often every two weeks or every month. They need to know that you are keeping track of it and that they will be held accountable for getting better. Again, this shouldn't be an issue with someone who genuinely wants to improve, but even motivated people can be helped by knowing someone is watching their progress. Adding a standing item to the one-on-one agenda is an effective way to remind yourself to check in.

Finally, make sure you celebrate their progress. This is terribly underused, but it's good to appreciate the work your team has put in to improve. Take them out for lunch, buy them a small commemorative trinket, or just call them out in front of the group. The specific thing you do doesn't matter nearly as much as the fact that you are doing it and recognizing them.

If They Aren't Motivated

If the employee is not motivated in their job, you need to decide if it's possible to get that drive back, or if the employee needs to leave. This will sound really harsh, and nobody wants to confront an issue that could result in upheaval like that. You likely don't want to consider it because you think you can fix them, they still do good work, and/or that's a conversation you don't want to have. The employee doesn't want to consider it either, for obvious reasons.

Nevertheless, it is a conversation you will have to have. Employees that don't want to be there and don't enjoy doing the work are not going to be worth your time. I've heard it said that four out of five times when you replace an employee, the new person is better. Based on my own experience, I fully believe that.

Firing someone is a very tough thing to do, and making the decision to do so is not something you want to take lightly. But many times it is the best option for everyone because both sides end up with a better fit. In an ideal world, an employee who isn't enjoying their job and would rather have a different one would just take the initiative and start looking for that new job. But most people aren't that proactive, and many would rather stay in a role they dislike and complain about it than take active steps to improve the situation. This is where your responsibility as a manager bears its full weight down on you, because they have handed responsibility for making that decision to you.

Before you fire anyone, you must work very closely with your employee to see if there are ways to get that motivation back, or if the lack of it is a temporary thing due to other circumstances, like their personal life. Sometimes people just get into a rut at work, and aren't being challenged. This can lead to extreme demotivation. Figure out if there are new challenges you can give to them, because tackling something new and fresh can be really invigorating. Really, you should be doing this with all of your employees no matter what their current motivation is.

Chapter 13

One-on-One Meetings

Welcome to your secret weapon for management.

I agree, this is perhaps the most underwhelming reveal of a secret weapon. After all, it's hardly rocket science. Talking with your employees privately about their personal and professional lives isn't a new concept, and you can't even pretend it's something you'd need to pay a consultant to figure out. Yet many companies do just that, and many more never even take that step. It's the most simple concept in the world, and one that you (hopefully) have already implemented in other areas of your life.

If you're married or dating seriously, you probably have special date nights where the two of you connect outside of the normal day-to-day routine. Many of us even do this with friends, albeit in an entirely different context. But we clearly recognize in our personal lives that this is an important facet of connecting with someone else, and having the time to sit down and talk is critical to keeping a relationship healthy and thriving.

For better or worse, you spend at least as much time around your team as you would a close friend, spouse, or significant other. The relationship already exists, so you have to decide if you want to invest in helping it thrive or if you want to let it wither. Investing in a relationship requires many different things, but the most important is dedicated time to spend together without outside influence.

There are a dozen different ways to structure this, and no one way is especially better than others. However, there are a few basic ground rules that are important to follow because they keep some structure and help the meeting actually achieve its purpose.

- The meeting should be scheduled on a regular basis. I prefer every two weeks for (up to) an hour, but some people adjust the meeting timing to as frequently as weekly or as infrequently as every three weeks, and cut the time down to half an hour. Once a month is a little too infrequent to be truly helpful.
- The meeting should be primarily focused on work concerns.
- The meeting should have a standard agenda.
- The meeting should require the employee to prepare before the meeting by filling out the agenda.
- The meeting should result in commitments to do something, and those commitments should be reviewed at the next meeting.

The ground rules will go a long way toward ensuring a productive meeting, but your behavior during the meeting is also critical. Here are some specific things you can do to give yourself a good shot at developing a strong personal relationship during these one-on-one meetings.

Some people like to include personal discussion in their meetings, while others prefer to keep it professional. If you would like to include personal matters, understand that not all of your employees will be comfortable sharing like that, so be understanding. Show you care, but don't pry.

You can also start by asking (or having them write), what is going well/poorly in work/personal life.

You may also want to ask them what they are doing to grow professionally. There is not one correct answer to this, but if they want to advance their career or skills, they should have identified something they can do to grow professionally.

Despite the benefits of getting to know your team personally, understand that you are their boss. Always keep it professional between your team and yourself, and treat each person equally.

You should be doing these things already as a decent person, but some things bear repeating. You are a boss, not a friend. Even if a friendship exists outside of the manager-employee relationship at work, there should be no doubt how it functions within the office.

What Are You Trying To Get Out of It?

One-on-one meetings are a great way to make sure that you are on the same page with the rest of your team, to check in on projects they're working on, and to keep up with them personally.

The most common and most immediately useful case for the one-on-one meeting is to discuss the nitty-gritty of work. You should be talking about the projects they're working on and how they are going. You may already be doing this for some projects and some people, even without a regularly scheduled one-on-one meeting. If that works well for those projects, then keep it going. But rarely are all projects treated like this, so these meetings are a good chance to review the stuff your team members are working on and to see where they're at or what help they need. This is where you can be helpful by asking the right questions, connecting them to people they need to talk to, or letting them know whether a task is especially important or urgent. There is no set way that this conversation needs to happen, but it does need to happen.

Talking about longer-term projects and professional development is also a great use of this time. If there are skills they want to develop, types of work they want to be doing, or just simply somewhere different they want to be in the future, you can help guide them there. This might be the biggest reason why one-on-one meetings are so helpful for both the employee and the manager. The employee is encouraged to think about how they want to grow, and the manager is helping coach that person toward that goal. If both sides are enthusiastic and committed to the goal, it will help your team to grow, and be a major reason why they enjoy working there.

One-on-one meetings are also a great time for your employees to bring up anything that has been bothering them lately or any questions. Having these meetings means you have opened up the line of communication for anytime they have an issue, question, or concern. But remember, these can be hard conversations! It's a secret weapon, but that doesn't mean it's always easy to manage or that you will always have the right answers.

When you do have these more difficult conversations, be as open and honest as you can. If they're unhappy with the type of work they're doing, having trouble with a coworker, thinking about leaving for another job, having troubles at home that are spilling over into work, or anything else, you want to make it a supportive and productive conversation. That doesn't mean that you automatically agree with everything they say or give them exactly what they want, but you can make these conversations easier with a thoughtful and supportive approach. Commit to listening and taking their concerns seriously. The result will be what it will be, but even the act of listening and taking them seriously can be very powerful.

Who Owns This Meeting?

The other key to making one-on-one meetings effective is that while you own setting it up, creating an agenda, and making sure that it actually takes place, this is not your meeting. This is the meeting for your team member and for them to help you understand what they're working on or dealing with.

However, you can't just sit back and be a silent participant. You will need to ask questions and try to uncover the things you don't understand, but if they want to use the time to talk about personal stuff, work stuff, or something else entirely, it's up to them.

You still have a voice, and you should use it if you think they are not meeting expectations in some way. If they aren't taking the meeting seriously or preparing for it well, you should call that out. It's not that different from managing them in a project. You need to give them the space and trust to do it well, but call them out if they aren't living up to expectations.

What If You Manage 10 Or More People?

This is a really hard one, and it does make these one-on-one meetings more difficult because you can't spend as much time with each person and still have time left in your day for your other responsibilities. Yet you can still meet with everyone. You will need to spend less time with each individual person and probably set them at a less frequent cadence.

Some people like to schedule all of these back-to-back so that it takes less switching time to move from working to managing, and that can be a helpful way to manage all of these meetings.

As an aside, keep this in mind as you begin to rise to a position where you have control over how the organization is structured. It is very difficult for one person to competently manage more than around eight people, and five is usually a more ideal number. Once you start moving above that, you just don't have enough time to truly connect with your team and understand their needs. You've probably had a manager who you felt didn't understand what you did, making your annual reviews cursory. You don't want to become this manager or for your company to be prone to having this type of manager, so making sure the employee-to-manager ratio is manageable is important.

Why These Meetings Are Critical

You have to be the manager that you would want. Nothing will damage a relationship more than a lack of understanding between manager and employee. A few relationships can get this regular one-on-one time naturally, through coffee breaks or ad-hoc meetings, but do not count on those to be a full replacement for consistent check-ins.

If you aren't already having them, you need to make regular one-on-one meetings a big priority. They're easy to put together, and while they can take up time, it's some of the most useful time you'll spend with your team. Problems get solved in these meetings, steam has a chance to be vented before it explodes, and you build a better relationship with your team and their work. Those benefits should be worth the handful of hours per week that you will need to invest.

Chapter 14

Managing Someone Whose Job You Can't Do

You may be tasked with supervising an employee or team that falls outside of your traditional area of expertise. Many managers are promoted from within and already understand most of the nuances of the work being done. This means that their primary skill gap is usually management skills. But if you are being promoted from one type of work to another, or if you need to supervise work you haven't personally done yourself, you will need to fill the management skill gap in addition to the newly identified technical skill gap.

There are some significant differences between managing a team you fully understand and one that is newer to you. For example, you probably won't be able to be much help with technical skills training for new employees if you're unfamiliar with their area of expertise. You will have a harder time estimating how long it will take to complete tasks. You may not be able to pitch in during crunch time. When hiring new members of the team, you will find the technical interview difficult, if not impossible.

However, all of these challenges are surmountable, as long as you have the right approach and (especially) the right attitude. You will need to be very curious and very humble. You will need to spend extra time studying up on at least the basics of the technical skills. You will need to be able to trust your team with a lot, and in turn earn their trust in your leadership ability.

Ultimately, being able to lead is not the same thing as being able to do every single job represented on your team. It's about making sure the team is moving in the right direction, getting the right things done at the right time, and continually improving.

This is what your job is now. Even if you have a dual role where you are still expected to contribute in a technical way, the management and leadership is the more critical and important part of your job. Without that, the team falls apart and breaks off into a thousand different uncoordinated directions. Your job is to bring them together in a unified direction; understand the broad purpose, strengths, and weaknesses of each skill and talent in your team; and put each resource to its best use.

Most generals can't personally fire each piece of artillery or pilot a fighter jet, but a capable general will understand what these pieces do well and be able to put together a plan for how best to use them together to accomplish an objective that each piece individually would not be able to achieve. You are in the position of a general, and you need to have this mindset.

Earning Trust

When you first join the new team or get the new employee, they may already know that you aren't as skilled as they are. If they don't, they will know soon. Nothing is more obvious than someone running from tasks they aren't able to do, or worse, trying to fake their way through them and doing them very badly.

I find that being up front and honest about the challenges you're facing can help. There are a lot of ways to do this, but usually a one-on-one setting is most effective. In a group setting, fewer individuals will ask questions or offer help, and you may have more people walking away from the meeting with doubts and questions. In a one-on-one meeting, you can read their reaction, and if they aren't already asking questions or offering support, you can dig a little deeper and ask how they feel about it. Most people are happy to help out and will do what they can to help you understand what they do.

This doesn't need to be a complicated discussion. Let them know that you don't have the depth of knowledge that they do, but you are committed to learning what you need to know, and to helping the team out in the best way you can. To do that, you'll need them on your side to help with decisions that require their expertise.

One of the best and most effective ways to earn trust is to demonstrate trust in others. Some people, when they feel a little out of their area of expertise, feel the need to micromanage everything. If you can pull back a little bit, let this person know what you need them to do and that you trust that they can find the best way to do it. Doing this help you significantly in building their trust in you. You will need to understand what they do and why it's important, but when you take their advice and trust their judgment they will put trust back in you.

But after trying this, what if you are still having trouble earning this trust with an employee? Some people are not especially willing to follow someone who has a different professional background than them, and this is especially prevalent when technical experts are led by non-technical people. Sometimes these relationships take time to build, so don't expect it to work perfectly on day one. Demonstrate to this person that the things you're good at will be helpful to them and that you can help make their lives easier. And if you can show trust in their technical ability and judgment, it will help them begin to trust you and your judgment.

Everyone is their own biggest fan, and experts are no exception. Simply put, being a good boss and being open and honest with them will help you build this trust.

Respecting Their Contributions

One big risk with managing someone whose job you don't fully understand is that you are prone to discounting their contribution, or not actively recognizing it as important. You know intellectually that what they do is valuable, but if you aren't seeing the actual ways in which it's helping the team you probably won't think about it very much.

This behavior is unintentional but problematic because it is usually clear to the other person that you don't understand their work. In a situation like this, they may begin to feel dissatisfied in their work. Would you want to work for a boss who didn't really understand what you did and couldn't be bothered to care? Don't let yourself be that boss. There will be times in your career when you are asked to manage someone who doesn't fit into your team perfectly, or to take over a team that has a different skillset than yours. Regardless of their specific skills, you need to treat them as important and have a good sense of what they do and why it is critical. You will know you have hit this spot when you can understand how they're going to approach a project and can provide useful feedback on their plan. You don't need to know the small details (although familiarity never hurts), but you do need to know how they do their job and why it's done that way.

Make sure that you are watching your attitude toward your team and not letting it slip into disdain for one person's role or skills. You need to have genuine respect for the work that they do, and make it clear that it's important. Sit down with them periodically to talk about what they're doing (this is where the one-on-one meetings come in handy) and how they think about their work. If it's not clear to you, then you have an opportunity to coach them in selling their highly specialized skills to an uneducated audience, with you as the guinea pig. If you show actual and sincere interest, it can be a great way to help them progress in their career (people in specialized roles often know that they are prone to being marginalized), and for you to have a greater understanding of your entire team.

Learning New Skills

If you are joining a team that does work you don't already understand, or does it using a tool you don't understand, then you need to spend dedicated time making sure you learn it. You do not need to be a master at it, but you need to understand what works well, what the challenges are, and be able to pitch in when necessary. Part of your job as a manager is to look for new opportunities to move the team forward, and you simply cannot do that if you don't understand the work that the team is doing. Some managers will try to do that, and it rarely works well. I've known coders who had managers suggest new tools that were so far from useful that the entire conversation was a waste of time. If you're managing a sales staff that sells a service, whereas you came from selling products, you will not immediately understand the differences in the sales process and will be a much less effective coach for your team for as long as you aren't closing that knowledge gap.

You will have limited time to learn everything, so you will need to use your judgment to determine the most important things to learn first. Is it more critical that you learn the specs of all your products or the standard pitch that your team uses to sell them? You'll eventually need to learn all of them, but if you want to get started quickly and be an effective manager early, then you will have to learn the most important things first.

This knowledge is best gained from your new team. Spend some time asking them for advice about the things that you will need to understand about their job. There is no shame in being curious and willing to admit you don't know everything. As long as you ask these questions honestly and openly, you will have a good shot at being an effective manager for your team.

Managing Experts Effectively

Despite these challenges and shortcomings, you can still be an effective manager in this situation. The primary ingredients needed don't change, they just need to be used in different amounts. You still need to care about your team and their development. You still need to help build a long-term vision for your team. You still need to understand how your team spends their time and whether that time is being used most effectively. You will not be the general who picks up a gun and charges into battle in this person's place, but you shouldn't be doing that anyway. Not having the option to do that makes a lot of people feel uncomfortable about their status and how they might be viewed by the team.

Don't be intimidated by your shortcomings and what you don't know or aren't able to do. You are in this role to use the team in the best way possible. Keep that in mind, and your direction clearly defined, and you will be a good manager.

Chapter 15

Compensating For Weakness

No matter who you are, no matter how long you have been working, and no matter how hard you try, you will always be bad at some things. Learning how to cope with this is important, and we will walk through some strategies for doing so.

The phrase "Impostor Syndrome" may already mean something to you. If not, it's essentially the feeling that you are inadequate for your job and that your lack of ability may be discovered at any moment. It's a feeling rooted in fear and anxiety, and is very common among certain high achievers. This is the feeling that we are going to try to identify and control during this chapter. It can be a useful impulse if it drives you to improve, but it can often morph into a perverse doubt of your abilities and feelings of anxiety.

Management has a tendency to expose every weakness you have, and to do so at the worst possible time. The more you can learn to control your reaction to this, the easier your life as a manager will be.

Be Honest About It

I have worked with too many people who are afraid to say that they can't do something well, especially when it's something that they "should" be able to do. I see this most often with people early in their careers. They want to be treated as an equal to someone with more experience, so they don't want to say anything that will make them look less qualified than that person. This is the bad side of "fake it till you make it," because it's usually pretty easy to tell when someone doesn't know what they're talking about and is just trying to look like they do. Don't be this person.

If you don't understand something, say so. If you don't know what a particular company does, ask someone to explain it to you. If you have no idea how to do something, ask for help. Most likely, you were good about this early in your career, but now you are trying to act like a boss who has it all together. Someone who has it together wouldn't need to ask for help, and knows everything already, so you don't want to have to ask for help.

Surprisingly, being open and honest about your shortcomings can actually make you look more credible in someone else's eyes. Certainly, being caught trying to fake something you don't know will damage your credibility. But asking for someone's help to understand it shows that you are working to get better, and it will actually allow you to build more trust with that person.

There does come a point at which you can be too honest, but usually this is less a problem with what you know and instead a problem with your willingness to learn and retain that information. You should understand the basics of your job well already. If you don't and are constantly having to ask for help and re-explanations of the same things, then you need to evaluate if you actually want to put in the work that it will take to be an effective manager. Knowing things is a very basic requirement, and if you aren't willing to put in that work, you will not be willing to do the more difficult things.

Work To Close The Gap

Of course, you should be trying to learn the things you don't know and are important to your job. You need to set an example for your team that they should be constantly learning new things and trying new approaches. It will also pay significant and obvious dividends for you because you will get better at your job.

For many of us, it's hard to even identify the countless things you may need to learn. Ask yourself the following questions to see if there are gaps that you are aware of but haven't completely closed yet. These are just a starting point, and you may have others that are helpful for you in finding those things you don't understand.

- Are there technical skills or tools important to your job that you don't really understand?
- Do you understand your competitors and their business strategy?
- Do you understand what the largest companies in your industry do, even if they aren't necessarily direct competitors?
- Do you frequently hear about certain concepts that you don't understand?

Write down your answers to these questions, and decide which ones you want to pursue first. They will probably all be ones you eventually work on, but you have to start somewhere.

Do some research on your own first, and see if you can find out what's been written about these things. In some cases, like newer technical tools, you will probably find a wealth of knowledge freely available. Take some time out of your day for researching these things. It will be a good use of your time.

In many other cases, the self-directed research will not get you very far. You can look at a competitor's website to try to understand their strategy, but useful information is rarely available there. Even if you do find information, it will probably not be written for someone trying to understand it as deeply as you are. You may find articles written by Wall Street analysts about this company's financial performance and how they're trying to increase sales in this segment, but it may not be especially relevant for you. You now need to get some human advice.

Let Others Help

Other people are going to be your best resource here. If you need to understand what a competitor is doing, you probably already know someone who can tell you. Most likely, they will be happy to tell you, too. People love feeling like an expert and sharing their knowledge, but most people are rarely asked for it. When you ask, they will probably be happy to share. Come prepared with the questions you want answers to, and be ready to learn.

If you are weak in a particular area but still need to demonstrate that your company understands it, recruit someone from your team who is an expert. There may be times when you need to be able to explain something to someone else, such as when you're on a sales call and the prospect has some deep questions about the technical side. It can be best to let them hear it from the horse's mouth instead of you trying to learn about it and then tell the prospect. This may sound really obvious, but some people have a hard time not being the expert. They will get themselves into trouble by suggesting they know a lot about a subject but then stumble when they're tested. Be humble, and ask for help.

Accept That You Can't Know Everything

As you put together the list of things you want to learn, you probably considered a few things that you didn't end up putting on the list. If not, then you either have a lack of curiosity or are overly ambitious. We'll hold off on the lack of curiosity for now, but the ambition can be a stumbling block if you're not careful. It's really easy to want to do everything and want to be an expert in everything. Our society encourages it; because information is so accessible, being uninformed can look like laziness. For someone with acute impostor syndrome, this fear of being lazy and uninformed can lead to some anxiety about what you haven't learned yet. You will look at other people who know what you don't know yet and fear that you won't get there. You need to be comfortable not getting there for everything.

Be comfortable saying that you don't know the answer to something rather than trying to fake your way through question after question. Use it as an opportunity to learn how they are thinking about problems and opportunities.

Part of being an effective leader is knowing your limitations and being comfortable with them. Everyone is impressed with the polymaths who seem to have the answers to every single problem, but that's usually more a function of big words and overconfidence than it is of greater knowledge. Confidence is great, but it doesn't always lead to helpful answers.

If your list is short and you didn't reject anything, you might need to expand your horizons or deepen your focus. There may be exciting new developments to problems you've already solved, different perspectives and approaches that you need to understand, or even just new companies in your space that you should be aware of. If you can't find anything you want to learn, look harder.

Humbling Yourself

Management is hard, and this is another example of how it will challenge you in fun and exciting ways. On the one hand, you are the leader who needs to understand broad trends and abilities, but on the other hand you are a human who couldn't possibly understand everything that exists in the world. You will get better at this in time, but it's an especially intimidating period early in your management career when your limitations and weaknesses are more easily exposed.

Don't be embarrassed by this, but embrace the fact that you are in the deep end and will learn how to swim quickly. Accept where you are at this moment, and humble yourself in front of others.

This is especially hard because it probably goes against some of what you have learned in your own career and from examples of others. Confident people and knowledgeable people get promoted, and you were probably one of these people when you were promoted. Now you are being asked to drop the confidence and be more humble. This is not the time to project an overly confident persona, because you don't know everything yet! And if you think you do, then go back to the beginning of this book and start over because you've clearly missed the entire point.

You will be good at some things at the beginning, and really bad at many others. Accepting the fact that you need to improve and learn more will make it easier and faster to actually improve and listen to coaching, or to seek advice. Thinking that you already know the answer, or were able to completely figure it out by searching your own mind and never asking anyone else is a mistake that will cost you dearly.

Be humble, accept that you don't know everything today but will get better, accept that you can never know everything but can learn how to find the answers, and be willing to ask others for advice and feedback. Do these things, and you will become a great manager of your team more quickly than you expect.

Chapter 16

Conflict Between Employees

Sometimes, two employees can't get along. It is a dramatic drain on morale, as the animosity between these two people makes things extremely difficult and stressful for everyone around them. You've probably worked around two people who couldn't get along and continually displayed that anger.

Since you're a leader in the company, you are responsible for letting them know that the unprofessional behavior is unacceptable and has to stop. They might think the impact is limited to just the two of them, but you will need to make it clear that the fight is like a black hole that swallows up the entire team's attention and energy in a really unproductive way.

These situations could pop up for any reason, and you will rarely be able to "solve" the underlying problem. If two people don't want to like each other, a third person such as their boss will not magically convince them to become best friends. The solution is ultimately up to them, because if they don't want to make it happen, then it will not happen. The most you can do is to give them a good reason to get along.

The best case scenario might be that the two learn to peacefully coexist, with occasional flare-ups. As long as you keep that in mind and don't try to play relationship counselor, you will have a shot at success.

Most conflicts are temporary, and people are able to quickly forget them. One person says something that the other person takes offense to, an apology is made, and the situation is over. Keep in mind that most conflicts will be exactly like this, and it's best to let them just play out. Offer a sympathetic ear and listen to anything your team brings you, but encourage your team to solve those issues by themselves. You want your team to be able to stand up for themselves and solve their own problems, and some people need to be told explicitly to do so. Give them advice as best you can, but don't offer to step in and help. Do offer to help if the situation doesn't get resolved. Most of the time, it will.

Eventually, there will be cases where the two just aren't able to resolve their problems. It might be one person's fault, it might be both, but either way it's on both of them to make an effort to resolve the situation. This is where you might be able to help by playing mediator. If you have an HR department that handles this stuff, great. If not, then it's likely that the responsibility will fall on you.

There are not a lot of different types of conflict, but there are some differences in the way you will be able to handle them. If both employees are under your management, you have certain options. If your team is having trouble with another team, you'll need to change the strategy somewhat. Finally, you might be having trouble between yourself and your own team, which is a different challenge.

Conflict Between Two Subordinates

In some ways, this is the most straightforward type of conflict to manage. They both report to the same person, you, who has a vested interest in making sure the situation gets resolved smoothly.

Of course, no situation like this is ever easy. By the time it has come to your attention, the relationship has likely already been strained for a while. There are no easy ways to make two people who get on each other's nerves like each other. Your goal is to get them to be able to deal professionally with each other.

If you haven't already, a good place to start is to get the whole story from each person privately. This is a good use of your one-on-one meetings, and they may have already talked to you about it there. What frequently happens is that only one person brings it up, so you will need to go get the story from the other person, too. Just listen, and don't try to solve everything right then and there.

If possible, try to watch their interactions too. Most of these tend to play out in public anyway, so get your own observation of what those arguments look like.

After you have the whole story, it's very likely that you will have two very different stories to compare and make sense of, and it will be very hard to do so coherently. People naturally see an argument from their perspective, especially when it's one that they haven't already resolved. Most likely, there will be fault from each side that you need to correct.

When you talk to each person, focus only on your conversation with them. They probably will want to know what you said or did to the other person. Don't go into any detail, other than sharing the fact that you've talked to the other person. You're not here to make one person feel better, you're here to get the two to get along. You want to keep it focused on the person you're talking to and the things they need to do.

Give them practical strategies they can use to defuse the situation next time. If they feel it getting heated, they can walk away. If they're really angry at the person, they can talk to you about it or go cool down in a private meeting room. Give them other resources they can use to help them deal with the conflict.

Do this with each person, and keep a very close eye on that relationship over the next few weeks. Give them some space away from each other if possible, but this should be temporary. You want to keep a harmonious work environment for everyone, but that doesn't mean you have to bend over backwards to keep those two apart. If they're bad enough and refuse to get better, you may need to fire one or (usually) both of them.

Conflict Between Your Team And Another Team

When your team is having an issue with somebody managed by someone else, you have more of a responsibility to make sure it gets resolved. Again, the first thing to do is see if the groups can resolve it on their own, but if that fails then you need to take it up with the other manager. Ultimately you need to help bring both parties to the table to resolve this.

These types of conflicts can be some of the worst and hardest to resolve, because the attitude frequently flows from the team leads themselves, and the individual conflicts are just a reflection of that. IT teams may look down on Account Management, so any time the two have to interact, sparks will flare up. As one of these team leads, you need to step in and try to solve the underlying issue.

Usually, the issue isn't that the teams actually dislike each other, but that something in the process is broken. Account Management may have a habit of making incredibly urgent last-minute requests, or IT may refuse to listen to constructive feedback from other teams on their projects. Look to see if you can understand why the tempers rise when these two groups interact, and see if there's a way to fix it. Usually in these cases a better or smoother process will go a long way, as long as both sides agree to use it.

There may just be a personal animosity between two people, despite the rest of the team interacting well. To the extent reasonable, you may consider shifting responsibilities to reduce the interaction of these two people. If you need to move roles, then move both people. If you move just one, it will look like a punishment for one and slap on the wrist for the other. Most likely, both are equally at fault.

Ultimately, you will probably have to get the two in a room, along with you and the other manager, and tell them point blank that they are going to have to get along. Don't let this be a session where they air their grievances (that happens privately), but firmly state what the expectation is, that it needs to start happening immediately, and that you will be watching.

Conflict Between The Team And You

This might be the trickiest to deal with, because you are no longer an observer, but an active participant. Hopefully someone has noticed and brought you to your senses well before this, but if not, you need to be able to recognize that you are part of the problem. Now is the time to practice what you preach and make sure that you are working to resolve the conflict rather than prolong it.

Arguments between superiors and their subordinates will look different than arguments between peers. The majority of folks won't do anything to argue with their boss, except in extreme circumstances. But the conflict can take different forms, usually less direct. You may be frustrated with a particular employee, and find yourself criticizing them more than others or not giving their work the same respect that you give to others.

Be the bigger person in this conflict. Acknowledge when you are wrong and being unfair. This is good not only in and of itself, but it will also help encourage the rest of your team to behave similarly.

Preventing Team Rot

Unresolved conflict is like a leaking pipe. Left unresolved, it will cause everything solid around it to rot through completely. A well-functioning team will fall apart if people in it start fighting or sniping at each other. You need to be aware of these things when they happen and make sure that everyone understands that it's unacceptable. Productive and constructive debate is great and should be encouraged, but acrimonious and hurtful argument is not. You will not be the one to solve most of these problems directly since you're just an outsider to the actual conflict. But you can make sure that you are pushing the team to resolve their issues, or to at least be able to work together professionally.

This is one of the less enjoyable aspects of being a manager and a leader because there are never any perfect answers, and you're trying to reconcile two people who have already made the decision to be angry at each other. If they don't want to get along, it will be much more difficult for you to handle. But this is why you are given the bigger title and the extra salary that comes with leadership: you have to deal with the most difficult and painful tasks. Hopefully you will never have so much practice resolving conflict that you become an expert at it, but it does get easier with time. Some people just need to be able to vent their frustrations about a person or situation in order to feel better or some other relatively harmless resolution. Work to find these types of creative answers to conflicts, and do your best. As long as you approach it without judgment, with a genuine desire to help and make the situation better, and a firm hand that makes clear you won't tolerate the situation going forward, you will have a good shot at success.

Chapter 17

When You Screw Up

To err is human. You've probably heard the phrase before. Since you're human, you will make plenty of mistakes while managing your team.

The difference between screwing up as an individual contributor and as a manager is one of scale. When you make a major mistake as an individual, it generally only affects you. When you're managing a team and you make a major strategic error, the entire team pays.

Despite the higher stakes, you will still make mistakes as a manager, and some of them will end up costing you dearly. You'll cause valuable employees to quit, or you'll end up wasting your team's time, or you'll poison the atmosphere by failing to fire an underperforming team member, or blunder your way into any number of innovative ways to cause trouble.

And it's okay. The point of your job is not to avoid screwing up - it's to correct those mistakes and make sure they don't happen again. If you alienate your team and cause some to quit, your job is now to repair relationships and build better ones. If you wasted time pursuing a bad strategy, now you have to listen to your team more closely when they warn you.

Recognizing Your Mistakes

This is not something most people do naturally. It is a skill you can develop over time, but you have to be willing to confront and acknowledge the fact that you are wrong or that you did something poorly. Most people don't want to do this. It is a skill that gets easier the more you practice it, but you have to intentionally practice it. You can't do it halfheartedly because it will be clear to everyone around that you don't really believe you made a mistake.

Don't blame others for your mistakes, even if they may have played a part in it. You may have gotten advice from someone that turned out to be wrong, or someone missed a deadline you were counting on them to hit. This is not to say that those things had no impact, but the point of this exercise is not to measure out each person's individual portion of blame and stick them with it. It's to see where we could have done better. Part of what you will need to do as a new manager is to hold others accountable for their mistakes, but you will not be able to do this effectively if you can't recognize the part you played in their mistakes. You may have ignored warning signs from them or failed to explain things fully. They may have even been primarily to blame for a larger mistake, but begin your search by looking at yourself to see what you could have done better.

In many cases you already know the major error that you made. If you hired the wrong person, you know the red flag that you saw but ignored. If you took an unnecessarily hard stance on a negotiation and the other side walked away, it's not hard to understand why. There isn't a lot of searching to do here.

Make sure that the obvious answer is actually the mistake that should have been fixed. Many times the first thing that comes to mind is just a decision made as a consequence of an earlier decision, and you really should be looking at fixing the earlier decision process instead. For example, if you hired the wrong person, but they were clearly the best available during your interview process, then part of what you need to recognize is that your process for getting good candidates to even apply isn't working. Many mistakes stand on their own, but you should consider the possibility that something you did earlier is also a cause of the problem.

A harder mistake to self-identify is reacting strongly over something that isn't life and death. It's a normal human reaction to be angry when someone does a poor job that negatively affects you. However, it's rare that this is a productive reaction. Your team will probably fix the issue you were yelling about, but they will most likely carry some significant resentment. Most people don't want to confront a situation like this, so you may not even explicitly hear that they reacted that way. You may still hold onto some of this anger, so it's hard to truly acknowledge that you were the one at fault for how you reacted. But be perfectly clear - this is bad judgment on your part and you are at fault. Yelling is very rarely the right way to react to problems, as it creates more problems than it solves.

One of the first and most important things to do when you've made a mistake is to acknowledge it. Don't try to hide behind excuses, even though some of them are probably valid, because they don't help clarify the situation. When you're acknowledging mistakes, look at the end result of your decision rather than your decision-making process. You will eventually need to go through the process by which you made the decision and see if you need to change anything there, but if you can't even recognize the result was bad, then you will not be able to improve the process.

Finally, don't beat yourself up about your mistakes. You have made mistakes before, and you will make them again. Look your mistakes in the face and acknowledge them, but don't dwell unproductively on them. Some people can't stop obsessing over what they could have done better, to the extent that they neglect to implement the changes needed to actually do it better next time. Recognize that you screwed up, and move on.

Triage

The first thing you need to do after making a major mistake is to ensure that the immediate consequences are taken care of. If you've screwed up a client call and left them unhappy, you need to begin the process of fixing that relationship. If you failed to test a code change and created bugs in the software, you need to get it back to working ASAP. This section will be short, because there isn't a lot to say that can apply generally, but don't lose sight of the fact that you will need to fix any immediate and urgent consequences of your mistake and cauterize the wound. Everything else in this chapter requires careful reflection and consideration, while this mainly requires action. Most likely, the action will be driven by others in your company who are acting like their hair is on fire, but realize that you may be this person to someone else. So give some thought to the best way of stopping the bleeding, which may not always be direct action. Some things just need time.

Postmortem

After you have acknowledged that you did not get the result you want and that you made an error, it's a good idea to think deeply about what you can do to prevent something similar happening in the future. In some cases, you needed to make a split-second decision, one that ended up being the wrong one. There may not be a lot you can learn from these, other than to improve your background knowledge of the issue so you can make better snap judgments. Other times, however, the decision drags out for longer, and the decision you made reflects the process by which you made it, for better or for worse. Since we're looking at acknowledging mistakes, let's assume it was for worse.

I've seen a lot of people fall into the trap of assuming that their decision-making process was great, caring little about the end result. This thing proposes that so long as you did the process correctly -and that's all you have control over - you shouldn't beat yourself up about a bad result.

There is some solid logic in this, but it's based on a potentially flawed premise. Is your decision-making process actually great? It's a really easy slight of hand to dismiss the end result as a fluke because the process worked as intended. Yet in doing so you neglect the most important part.

You need to constantly reevaluate the process by which you

made that decision. Most likely, there are many places where you could have caught the mistake early, before it became a real issue. Are you asking the right questions in your interview? Are you running all the tests you need to before pushing data to production? Spend some time walking through each step of your process to see if it's necessary and if there is anything you can add or remove to better catch those mistakes ahead of time.

And if you find no flaws in your process and you were truly the victim of rotten luck? Congratulations, you win. Go buy yourself a Coke.

Implementing Fixes

After you've looked through your process and decided where you can do better next time, you need to actually prepare for next time. This step is often neglected, because "next time" is often far enough away that it feels unnecessary to begin preparing for it. By the time "next time" comes around, you will most likely have forgotten the hard-won details and fixes you've found during this process. So make sure that you have a way to look back on what you've learned and actually implement the lessons. Write it down in a note that you'll come back to, write down what the new process will look like so you can use that as a reference next time, or whatever works best for you, as long as you are making intentional plans not to forget what you've learned.

Also make sure that you are reviewing the fixes with somebody else. Exactly who that is will depend on the particular mistake and who it affected, but generally you would work with your boss or your team. If you're working on your attitude toward your team and a tendency to treat them unfairly, you will want to walk your team through your fixes. If you're reviewing a bad hiring decision you made, that would be best handled with your boss. If it's a very sensitive subject or you need an outside opinion, talk to a mentor who doesn't work with you. These can sometimes be hard to get right, because your mentor won't understand the nuances of the situation like someone on your team would, but the new perspective can be invaluable.

Finally, go out and make an effort to get better by actually doing these things. Check yourself periodically during the "next time" and see if you are actually improving like you'd hoped. Some of the fixes probably won't work as well as you thought they would, so throw those out and replace them with new ones. You want to set the example of continuous improvement in your team, and this is a great place to demonstrate that.

Final Thoughts

You will never be perfect, but you can still be a good example of how to handle mistakes. The key is to be willing to acknowledge them without shame and to commit to getting better. You don't need to beat yourself up in order to recognize your own mistakes, but a clear-eyed self-evaluation will pay significant dividends. Your team will respect you more, your boss will trust you more, and you will become better for it.

It is an odd truth that calling attention to your errors will reduce their impact. You are rarely the only one who noticed the error because usually an error worth recognizing is one that is affecting multiple people. There is no hiding from it because it's already having an impact on other people. If you try to hide your mistake or your responsibility for it, it will be obvious.

Use your own life and opinion as an example. When you see people making excuses for their own errors or blaming other people, you usually lose respect for them and their decision-making process. Don't be this person, and take full responsibility for any part you may have played in a bad situation. It often takes swallowing your pride, but you will not regret being the one who takes ownership of the error.

Once you've done this, also make sure you are actually making the changes necessary to prevent it happening again in the future. This is another difficult thing for many people to do, because talking about making changes is much easier than actually doing the hard work of changing your behavior and attitudes. Don't neglect this, otherwise your team will see right through you and your empty words.

If you can do all of this well, you will have conquered one of the great challenges of being a manager, and one that most people have a hard time getting right. You will build respect among your team and encourage them to take the same responsibility by following your example.

Chapter 18

What To Do With Newfound Free Time

There will come a point in time when you have successfully delegated work, trained and empowered your team to make most battlefield decisions, and set clear goals for the team to work toward. At this point, you might find yourself with seemingly little to do. Your team is able to handle many of the day-to-day tasks and is probably already doing them better than you did when you worked on them. What do you do with the extra space that you've created in your day?

Start thinking about the long-term strategic questions facing your team.

Graduating from focusing on the day-to-day to focusing on longer term strategic questions can be really difficult. Not only are there no clear answers, but usually there aren't even clear questions. All that you know is the way things currently work and some of the more urgent issues within the team and the company. But there is no foolproof guide to tell you the best way that things could work in the future, or which issues are most important to solve first.

To give an example, you are the manager of a well-functioning IT team, and you have trusted deputies who can handle most of the daily workload without trouble. You are not spending much time working on daily problems, so you have started looking at the department as a whole to see how it needs to evolve.

You should start by looking for questions to answer. Does the team have the right skills? Does the tech stack need to be different? Does the team need to rebuild a system for tracking bugs in the code? Is the team large enough to handle everything? Are you keeping your most talented employees, or are they leaving? Are there new features to the product or process that need to be created?

Each of these questions will have dozens of potential answers, and it is not a simple task to even evaluate which questions need to be answered first. This is your responsibility as a manager and a skill that takes time and practice to develop. As you find yourself confronted with these questions, the first and most important thing you should do is to find a mentor who you can talk to about all of these questions and their potential answers.

Advice From Others

Having a mentor you can rely on is a huge asset. They're someone who can help you learn from their mistakes, propose better approaches to problems, and be a neutral sounding board for ideas. If you haven't done so already, finding mentors is a great idea, and that goes double for a new manager. You will have many things that you want and need to learn, and your boss may or may not be best suited to help you with all of those. At the very least, a mentor will be able to give you a fresh perspective and show you how they have handled issues in the past.

Take some time with your mentor at coffee or lunch and talk to them about what you see as potential opportunities within your team and things you have seen that are causing trouble or could be done more efficiently. Most likely, you already have some idea of better ways to do them, and run those ideas by your mentor as well. Get their opinion on those ideas, and ask to see if they have run into these problems before. If they haven't, or you aren't finding their answers helpful, try another mentor in your network who may have more applicable experience. If they do, do your best to understand their thought process, why they arrived at that plan, and how the implementation went. Are there things that they would do differently in hindsight? Are there other ideas they wish they had considered or attempted or have seen other companies try? This is a chance to learn, so after you have laid the groundwork for the conversation, you should be spending a lot of time listening rather than talking.

You then need to adapt their answers to fit you and your team. Use them as fertilizer for your own ideas, rather than adopting them wholesale. If an idea seems useful, take the useful parts and weave them into a plan that fits you and your team. Even if an idea seems bad or the main thrust of the idea is unworkable, there are likely useful parts that you can still use. Take those, and keep them in mind as you try to create your own answers. This is a key part of being a leader - taking and dissecting ideas and answers from others to arrive at a more effective answer for your team.

Finding The Questions

As a leader, you need to be constantly looking for ways to improve your process or efficiency. The biggest difference between being a leader and a follower is that suddenly people are looking to you to point them where to go. And most of the time, especially at the beginning, you won't have a clear idea of what the best approach is or where to point everyone. Your team will probably have dozens or hundreds of things that they could do and make better, but they will never have enough time to take care of them all.

If you read that last sentence carefully, you'll realize that it's predicated on having a lot of ideas for how to change things and deciding which one is best to work on right now. This is the way a lot of teams work because those answers are usually readily accessible and work can be started on them quickly.

A better way to make sure that your team is working on the right things at the right time is to instead start by looking at the right questions. For example, you may know that the script the sales team follows needs to be updated and rewritten, the expense submission system needs an overhaul, and the one-page document your team leaves with prospects could be better. But these are all answers to unasked questions, and you will be well served by trying to uncover the questions that you're trying to answer with them, as well as other questions that have been left unasked because no easy answers have been apparent. In the example above, you may not be converting as many prospects to sales as you need to, and you might be wasting a lot of your team's time on bureaucratic tasks.

As you begin trying to ask the underlying questions, also think about the other areas where you think an improvement could be made. Even if you don't have an answer available today, the question is still just as important as the others, and possibly even more important.

Once you've defined the right questions to be asking, you need to weigh them and see which ones are most important to answer. This is another exercise that is good to do alongside someone else, whether that's a boss, mentor, colleague at the same level, or trusted subordinate. The decision is ultimately yours, but a second mind can do a lot to sharpen your thoughts and make sure the final result is better.

Finding The Answers

This is another field where it can pay big dividends to think on the questions for a few days. Rarely does a big decision require speed, and speed can often lead to a lower quality decision. Even in the cases where speed is necessary, there is usually ample evidence ahead of time to identify the impending decision. If you find yourself with an employee who has done something so unacceptable that you need to fire them on the spot, you were probably well aware already that they were capable of putting you in that position, and hopefully you had thought ahead of time about how you would handle such a situation if it arose. Likewise, you should be thinking about how you would deal with any contracts you're currently negotiating if you had to make a sudden decision.

You will often find yourself in situations that you haven't

specifically prepared for, but you can still work to prepare yourself for the situations you think could come up. Plans are useless, but planning is critical.

How would you handle it if you suddenly signed a client that doubled your revenue, and you launched in half your normal timeline? Where would you go to find your next employee if you needed someone in a week? What if your company database is hacked and confidential documents leaked? There is no way to thoroughly plan for all of these things, but a good leader should at least be spending part of their time walking through these hypothetical situations because there will not be time to think clearly when the emergency hits.

As you do this, don't try to plan a very specific course of action for these specific, hypothetical scenarios. It's better to consider a host of options and their pros and cons because most likely the situation you actually end up confronting will be very different in the details than the situation you've created in your head, and having a variety of options will let you pick and choose the best pieces of each.

When you are confronted with the real situation, this preparation will only help. As others are running around with panicked looks on their faces trying to process the deluge of information, fears, possibilities, and risks, you will be a few steps ahead. And if the situation is less urgent than that (and they almost all are), you will still be in this advantageous position.

Talk to different people to get their opinion on your course of action, and take their input seriously. This is not a debate but rather a chance to learn. If it is truly your decision to make (and you should establish early whether or not that is the case), then there is no debate to be had, just open dialogue. You can and should listen to good advice, otherwise you will likely make a lower quality decision that has a higher chance of being wrong and will not have a base of support other than your own.

Thinking Strategically

None of the advice I have given here is related to the actual substance of the answer; those details will be specific to you. But I can show you better ways to work on your decision-making process.

After you have started looking at the questions that you need to answer, and have identified the two or three that are most critical to your success, spend the next few days thinking about them and sketching out ideas. Don't pressure yourself to arrive at a final answer, but make a special effort to consider multiple possibilities. This process of picking the question up and putting it back down over a period of days (and sometimes weeks/months) can be very helpful to sharpen your thinking. Eventually, as your comfort with the different answers grows, you will find yourself drawn primarily to one or two particular answers. In a lot of cases, these are the answers you first thought of, but you will frequently surprise yourself and have a significantly better final answer as a result of this process.

Finally, this is a skill you have to practice actively. You will have a few successes with this process, assume you have mastered the skill, and put it down, only to find that your decision-making is again suffering. This is a skill that takes time, effort, and persistence. You will never be perfect at it, but you can at least be confident that you have followed a sure process and made the best possible decision based on what you knew at the time.

Chapter 19

Finding Your Replacement

As you manage people, you will confront the fact that you will probably not be in that role forever. You will decide to move on to another company, get promoted, or move to a different department or type of role in the company. No matter how you get there, your team will at some point need to be led by someone else, and you need to start trying to find out who that person is as soon as you can.

Hiring someone from outside is frequently a good idea, since you don't always have the perfect skillset available in your company. If you left today, that would probably be the case for your role. But if you were able to find, train, and put a person up as your logical replacement, then suddenly your options open up. Your boss probably fears trying to find someone to replace you, and that fear can work with you or against you. It can work with you if you simply want to keep what you have and avoid being fired. It works against you if you want to do something different than what you're doing now. Think about your own team - would you willingly move a talented team member who would be a significant challenge to replace? Most likely, your boss is not thinking about your career in those narrow terms, but that does give them a reason to think twice about moving you.

Likewise, if you decide to move to another company, it would be very difficult to leave on good terms without a quality replacement lined up. A big part of your career consists of your network, and leaving a company with bad feelings like that can cause problems that will affect you later.

Both of these problems go away if you have a talented and capable replacement already lined up. More likely, your options actually increase because you are seen as a manager with a good team and a logical succession plan. Your bosses will see that, and you will have many opportunities given to you because you have shown good judgment and forward thinking. You will not have a problem staying or leaving if you have a good replacement lined up.

Finding Them

The first and most important part of finding a potential replacement is to actually find that person. No brainer, right? Yet a lot of managers never even take this first step and have a set of employees who are indistinguishable from each other. You need to make a special effort to know that you have this person in house.

If you have yet to hire this person, you may need to wait until the next position opens up on your team. Once it does, however, you need to approach this hire a little bit differently. Instead of simply reviewing candidates solely in light of whether they would do a good job at the role being hired, you need to also evaluate their aptitude for eventually moving up in the company. This is not easy - it's difficult enough to make a quality hire for a well-defined role, much less trying to fit the person into a potential future role that is years away from reality. But you need to make an effort because it will pay off dramatically.

You may be fortunate enough to already have this person on your team. You may even be so lucky as to have two or more capable of eventually filling your shoes. If you aren't sure, or even if you are, the following questions will help separate the worthwhile candidates from the rest and decide where to focus some of your time.

- Is this person responsible? Can I count on them to follow through without supervision?
- Is this person honest? Do they make an effort to do the right thing, even when it's difficult?

- Is this person capable of surprising me? Do they frequently find different or better solutions that you haven't considered?
- Is this person willing to do the job? Would they want to rise to the occasion or are they happy where they are?

Training Them

When you have your person identified and on your team, you need to make sure that you are equipping them with the tools they will need eventually to do your job. Everything you have learned from this book, you need to try to impart to them. Some things will be easier than others, and some things are hard to learn without experience, but make an effort to show them how to do the things that you do and how you think about the team.

Part of giving them the tools to succeed you is in delegating work and responsibility to them. Not in deciding that you should or that it would make sense but in actually giving them the freedom to figure out how to solve a problem and the freedom to fail while doing so. Obviously you need to make these all happen within the limits of where the business can support failure - having a bad client call is a normal and supportable failure, but creating and working on a six-month project that was misguided from the beginning is different.

Encourage them to think like a manager and give them this responsibility explicitly. Have them help with managerial tasks, where appropriate. If you are hiring new members of their team, bring them on board for the process. Ask them to have input on some of the bureaucratic things you need to create as a manager, like interview questions and job descriptions. You want to get them thinking like a leader and comfortable with that mindset.

Keeping Them

The tricky thing about hiring talented people who are capable of moving up an organization quickly is that every other company is looking for those same people. Most likely, your team will have other opportunities that could cause them to leave. You've probably had the same, and while you made the decision to stay, other people may not do the same.

To keep your talented people, you need to give them good reasons to stay. Salary and hope of future promotion are not enough. You need to make it so that when they are confronted with the decision of whether to stay or leave, it is clear that their best future comes from staying with the company.

For starters, you need to be a good boss - a strong leader, but not a tyrannical one. This is not to say that you need to be deferential and meek to your team but you need to lead. Be someone they want to follow and makes them better. It also helps to have them working on interesting projects. Every role has the "ditch-digging" part of the job, the thankless and difficult tasks that nevertheless still need to be done. To balance those, encourage and clear the way for your team to work on bigger and more interesting projects or take advantage of growth opportunities as well. These are the types of things that go a long way in keeping talented employees engaged and enthusiastic. Talk with your people to understand where they want to grow and find those opportunities for them.

Despite all of this, you still may lose a great employee. This can be a really painful blow because of all of the investment plans you had, but life doesn't always move in a straight line. You occasionally have to do things over again even though you didn't make any mistakes the first time. Hopefully you have built a strong enough relationship that you can talk with your employee and try to understand why they are leaving. It's even better if the relationship is solid enough that they have been talking to you about the possibility they will leave as it's happening rather than after they have accepted another job.

You might be able to convince them to stay, and it's probably a good idea to try, but most of your work in this realm has already been done. A pay raise might keep them there, but that does raise the issue of why it took them threatening to leave to make the bump happen. If you are serious about keeping them, you need to be diligent about keeping up with their market rate to avoid this kind of situation.

If they do leave, try to stay on good terms rather than stomp your feet and rage about betrayal. You will probably run into them again or need their help with something, so thank them for their time and offer any help you can. It will hurt, and you will likely need to start over, but life sometimes happens that way.

Promoting Them

Part of having a talented employee is that they will be ready for a promotion or promotions quickly, and you will need to be aware of and manage this. This is absolutely a net benefit because having an employee grow into a new and more responsible position is good for all parties.

Sometimes the perception of whether someone is ready to be promoted is different between the manager and the employee. With reason, the employee may feel like they're ready for more responsibility (and more pay), while the manager may have a strong grasp on their weak points and some of the challenges they will face if given additional responsibility today. Do not assume that these challenges would resolve quickly if they were promoted. Being given too much responsibility too quickly can be a negative if someone is not ready to rise to the challenge. People can be overpromoted and not have the tools to handle the extra challenges that come with it, and this can lead to bad habits, loss of confidence, or coping mechanisms that cause additional problems. In an extreme case, they may be so unprepared for the new job that the company cannot afford to keep them there and they need to be let go.

One of your roles as a manager with a talented employee is to be in constant communication with them and honest about their weaknesses. If there are problems you see that they need to work on before they can be promoted, you have to let them know what they are and work alongside them to help them address those problems. Have these conversations during your one-on-one meetings, and also get their thoughts on their own weaknesses. These will usually line up well with what you think, but there's a good chance you'll be surprised by one or more of their self-identified weaknesses. Whether or not you agree completely with those weaknesses, they are also worth adding to the list of things to work on.

This can cause friction among other employees if they see someone moving up the ladder at a faster pace than they are. Personally, I'm a little less sympathetic to this concern than other people - either someone is ready for a promotion or they aren't, and other people shouldn't have an impact on the decision to promote them. Regardless, this may be a headwind that you run into, and you will need to navigate it carefully to avoid causing problems with your peer managers. Generally, you want the rationale behind the promotion to be obvious to the larger company. Other people should have worked with the newly promoted employee and know their dedication and the quality of their work, and you should be singing their praises far and wide as well. It should not come as a surprise to anyone to see them get promoted.

What If You Have More Than One?

As much work as it is to find and train a backfill employee for yourself, you may run into the pleasant challenge of having two or more talented and qualified candidates. It's a great feeling to have a deep bench of talent that you can deploy, but it also can cause some other challenges that you will have to navigate.

One of the main challenges is that each of them may personally feel like they're fighting for the same position, and thus any advancement by the other person is seen as blocking their progress. This is an awful feeling to create in your team because the focus moves from how each person can succeed to measuring how they are doing against each other. Real world jobs are not the Olympics where there can only be one gold medal winner. There are usually multiple paths open to any one person, and having two or more qualified people available just means that you can populate more of those paths. It is true that two people can't always be promoted into the same role at the same time. After all, there is only one CEO. But one of your tasks is to make the different paths clear and obvious to your team, and avoid putting them into direct competition for what they think are scarce resources. This ultimately only leads to resentment.

You need to find the unique path that will best take advantage of their tendencies and skills. Each employee is unique in their strengths and weaknesses, so there will be some roles that fit certain people very well and some roles that fit others well. Don't just think your Type A employees are your leaders. This, in particular, is a fallacy and can lead to negative results if you aren't careful. Many people with Type A personalities are less suited for leadership than would be expected because they have the confidence but lack much of the skill required. However, other personality types can often be fantastic fits for a leadership role. Know your people, and make your decisions accordingly.

Having A Great Replacement

It is very hard to find a talented employee who can be trained to replace you. It takes diligent and thoughtful work to find them, train them, and keep them. This is a job that you should begin working on as soon as you can because it is not something that will happen quickly or easily, and it can take years to have someone fully ready to take your spot. Having a ready replacement will give you significantly more options in your career and will help advance that talented person in their own career. The world is littered with bosses who made great contributions but failed to find a capable successor. Don't be one of them.

Chapter 20

The Challenge Of Management

Management tends to get a bad rap. The term "Game Manager" is a pejorative when applied to a quarterback, since it usually applies to someone who only does what is required of them and rarely rises to true stardom. Likewise, nobody grows up wanting to be a band manager. They would rather be the artist creating than the person doing the dirty business of booking shows, making sure the band is getting paid, and generally being the adult in the room. Name a manager in a book or movie, and I'll bet you that person is not the hero of the story. At best, they're a benign presence who serves as story filler.

So why would you want to be a manager?

Sure, people generally want to be promoted to manager, and you probably look up to many of the managers that you work with, but most people don't actually want to do the work of managing. Face it, you probably just wanted a promotion rather than to do everything detailed in this book. Actual management is often a thankless task because you get the blame if things go wrong and don't typically get the credit when they go well. This is the life that you are signing up for. Yes, it usually comes with a better paycheck (although some companies are starting to rethink this), but the actual work that you have to do is tough, thankless, and is always vulnerable to hindsight bias.

If you really want to manage people and do it well, you need to embrace all of the challenges. This will take you years of practice to become even decent at. You will not get there unless you love the actual day-to-day practice of getting better at management. This can be difficult when you are stuck in the middle of another thankless challenge, but you have to keep that love of the practice in mind.

Some of you may consider yourself so driven to succeed that you think your drive can carry you through these tough times. Trust me, it won't. Even if it could, you would be miserable and continually banging your head against the wall. Many people think they can power through this stage and end up quitting after a few years with no clear progress. Or worse, they stay despite never learning how to actually manage people well. To stay in this role and truly thrive in it, you need to embrace the fact that you have been given an incredible opportunity. Not just for yourself and your career, but a chance to help others.

You, who have worked hard to move up the ladder, but probably also benefited from some good management, advice, and leadership, have the opportunity to be that person for someone else. Think about what you could have done to help the younger version of yourself rise even faster or correct glaring errors more quickly. Now you are in the position to give other people an opportunity that they haven't fully earned yet and watch them take advantage of it to move further faster.

Think about all of the bad management you have encountered in your career. What are the mistakes that you saw coming from a mile away but couldn't convince someone to change their course? What about the employees who should have been corrected or fired years ago? You have the chance to be the voice in the room making those decisions, and making them in the right way and with ample deliberation. You can and will make your team the best-functioning team in the company. One where people are hesitant to leave, and you feel guilty hiring any one employee because that means you have to tell multiple other fantastic candidates that they didn't get the job.

Before you puff yourself up too much, also stop and humble yourself. Many of the managers you have criticized probably also saw the same errors in their own managers before they were promoted. Recognizing problems is much easier than being responsible for solving them. In many cases, you will have no idea how to fix a problem and sometimes even how to identify it. Yet you still are the one responsible for making sure it gets fixed. You will spend time and energy coming up with a solution that is a magical mix of input from others and your own inspiration, and you will see that solution fail. You did your best, and in hindsight there was something you could have done better, but you had to solve it with the information and skills you had at the time.

Understand that this will also happen to you, and being promoted into a role like this means that you will get criticized for making poor decisions. Not "you might get criticized." You will get criticized. Your mistakes are suddenly much more exposed because they now affect other people. You will feel like you are doing your best, yet still it will sometimes not be good enough. Keep this in mind as you start your journey, and learn to anticipate and accept this responsibility. Sometimes the buck stopping with you means that it really stops with you.

This is the paradox that you have to deal with while you're a manager. You are the leader, and you often need to inspire people to follow you. This is close to impossible if you don't believe in your cause 100 percent. You sometimes have to be the cheerleader for your team, even when the game looks lost, because the minute you lose hope you've lost your team.

Yet at the same time, as you push yourself to be positive and appeal to a higher ideal, you have to also understand that you will take the blame and give the credit. Management is rarely a star-making role, so if you need that kind of affirmation and attention in your life, then you need to either find that in a nonprofessional area of your life, or find a different career path.

Have I scared you away from managing yet? If so, good. Go do something else with your energy because the few hours you've spent reading this book have saved you years of fruitless toil. Consider it one of the best investments of time you've ever made.

If you are still convinced that this is the right path for you, then I also hope that this time has been helpful for you. You have seen the risks and still decided that the juice is worth the squeeze. But despite the fact that you will hit those same potholes and struggle just as hard as anyone else who tries to manage people, you will have the advantage of being able to anticipate the difficulties and steel yourself before they happen. You will screw up in ways you can't undo. You will see other people get credit that you deserve. You will get the blame for stuff that isn't really your fault. But you have accepted that this will happen, and you will be better for having gone through the trial.

As a new manager, your transition to this role is going to be one of the most difficult challenges you have ever faced because the challenge will be unique to anything else you've done before. But leadership alone cannot make things happen. Great individual contributions almost always pale in comparison to the scale of the task they're working on and at best will only solve a portion of the problem. If the problem is worth solving, then it needs more than one person solving it. Management is the forgotten link between these two necessary components of progress and might be better described as the hinge that both depend on. Be the best manager you can, and you will be the reason that both the individual contributor and the company as a whole succeed. If you want a place where your effort will be magnified, you have found it. I wish you the best.

Author Biography

Mikil Taylor is the VP of Analytics at Healthcare Bluebook in Nashville, TN. Like most new managers, he was thrown into the flames to learn how to manage a team. After years of struggle, and by combining his own positive and negative experiences with the advice that actually works in the real world, he has built a thriving team that won the Nashville Technology Council's "Team of the Year" award. Mikil has a passion for helping other new managers avoid the most common pitfalls in their new role, and his focus on demonstrating how to start with a solid foundation, molding the team, and, yes, dealing with the mistakes everyone inevitably makes, will give any new manager the tools they need to also build a successful team.

Note to Reader

Thank you for purchasing and reading *The Beginner's Guide to Managing*. If you enjoyed the book, an online review would be greatly appreciated, as reviews help to spread the word to others who this book may be able to help. If you would like to keep up with future projects, please visit MikilTaylor.com, where my blog expands on the theme of this book.

Sincerely,
Mikil Taylor

BUSINESS
BOOKS

Business Books

Business Books publishes practical guides
and insightful non-fiction for beginners and professionals.
Covering aspects from management skills, leadership and
organizational change to positive work environments, career
coaching and self-care for managers, our books are a valuable
addition to those working in the world of business.

15 Ways to Own Your Future
Take Control of Your Destiny in Business and in Life
Michael Khouri
A 15-point blueprint for creating better collaboration, enjoyment,
and success in business and in life.
Paperback: 978-1-78535-300-0 ebook: 978-1-78535-301-7

The Common Excuses of the Comfortable Compromiser
Understanding Why People Oppose Your Great Idea
Matt Crossman
Comfortable compromisers block the way of anyone trying to
change anything. This is your guide to their common excuses.
Paperback: 978-1-78099-595-3 ebook: 978-1-78099-596-0

The Failing Logic of Money
Duane Mullin
Money is wasteful and cruel, causes war, crime and dysfunctional
feudalism. Humankind needs happiness, peace and abundance. So
banish money and use technology and knowledge to rid the world
of war, crime and poverty.
Paperback: 978-1-84694-259-4 ebook: 978-1-84694-888-6

Mastering the Mommy Track
Juggling Career and Kids in Uncertain Times
Erin Flynn Jay
Mastering the Mommy Track tells the stories of everyday working
mothers, the challenges they have faced, and lessons learned.
Paperback: 978-1-78099-123-8 ebook: 978-1-78099-124-5

Modern Day Selling
Unlocking Your Hidden Potential
Brian Barfield
Learn how to reconnect sales associates with customers and unlock hidden sales potential.
Paperback: 978-1-78099-457-4 ebook: 978-1-78099-458-1

The Most Creative, Escape the Ordinary, Excel at Public Speaking Book Ever
All The Help You Will Ever Need in Giving a Speech
Philip Theibert
The 'everything you need to give an outstanding speech' book, complete with original material written by a professional speech-writer.
Paperback: 978-1-78099-672-1 ebook: 978-1-78099-673-8

Readers of ebooks can buy or view any of these bestsellers by clicking on the live link in the title. Most titles are published in paperback and as an ebook. Paperbacks are available in traditional bookshops. Both print and ebook formats are available online.
Find more titles and sign up to our readers' newsletter at
http://www.jhpbusiness-books.com/
Facebook: https://www.facebook.com/JHPNonFiction/
Twitter: @JHPNonFiction